Effective Primary Teaching

research-based classroom strategies

Edited by
Paul Croll and Nigel Hastings

David Fulton Publishers
London

David Fulton Publishers Ltd
The Chiswick Centre, 414 Chiswick High Road, London W4 5TF
www.fultonpublishers.co.uk

First published in Great Britain in 1996 by David Fulton Publishers

David Fulton Publishers is a division of Granada Learning Limited, part of Granada plc.

British Library Cataloguing in Publication Data
A catalogue record for this book is available from the British Library.

ISBN 1-85346-394-9

Typeset by Textype Typesetters, Cambridge
Printed and bound in Great Britain

Contents

Notes on Contributors

Rosemary Ayles is Head of the Department of Education Studies and Management at the University of Reading.

Paul Croll is Bulmershe Professor of Education in the Department of Education Studies and Management at the University of Reading.

Maurice Galton is Professor and Dean of Education at the University of Leicester.

Nigel Hastings is Professor and Dean of Education at the Nottingham Trent University.

Diana Moses is a Research Fellow in the Department of Education Studies and Management at the University of Reading.

Josh Schwieso is Senior Lecturer in Psychology at the University of the West of England.

Rhona Stainthorp is Lecturer in the Psychology of Education in the Department of Education Studies and Management at the University of Reading.

Kevin Wheldall is Professor and Director of the Special Education Centre, Macquarie University, Sydney, Australia, and Visiting Professor in the Department of Education Studies and Management at the University of Reading.

CHAPTER 1

Teachers Matter

Paul Croll and Nigel Hastings

Introduction

In this book we are concerned to bring the findings of educational research to bear on the practical problems faced by teachers in primary school classrooms. We take as our starting point a number of claims which we shall develop in more detail in this chapter and in Chapter 10.

1. Teachers matter: what teachers do makes a difference to the classroom experiences of themselves and their pupils and, through these, to the outcomes of education.
2. Any attempt to improve education must concern itself with outcomes, broadly defined. We have included the term 'effective' in our title because it focuses us on the effects of teaching and on the importance of finding ways to describe and measure these effects.
3. There is now a body of educational research which provides evidence on the relationship between teaching behaviour and educational outcomes and which is highly relevant to the practical day-by-day decisions which teachers must make in classrooms. These studies are robust in the sense of being consistent, generalisable and widely replicated.
4. There is no evidence to suggest that there is a single 'best' approach to teaching and teaching approaches will always need to be flexible, both with regard to the needs of particular classroom situations and the strengths and preferences of individual teachers. However, the notion of teaching *strategies*, a repertoire of types of approach supported by evidence on their consequences, provides a way in which research results can inform decisions about which strategies might be most fruitful in particular circumstances.
5. Teaching situations have important aspects in common and it is therefore possible to take lessons from one situation which are applicable to another. Doing this in a systematic and generalisable fashion is one of the purposes of educational research.
6. Teaching is more than a skilled activity or practical accomplishment.

> It is also a thoughtful activity which demands considerable intellectual engagement and reflective and self-critical analysis. It is a premise of this book that such analysis is best conducted in the context of an awareness of the widest range of research evidence on the consequences for educational outcomes of different types of classroom practice.

In the chapters which follow, the contributors consider the research evidence for effective primary classroom teaching in a variety of areas. Some of these are concerned with questions of overall strategies within the primary classroom for managing teaching and learning. Consequently there are chapters dealing with classroom organisation (especially the organisation of classroom seating), patterns of teacher interaction with pupils (especially the balance of whole class, small group and individual interaction), strategies for behaviour management, approaches to pupil motivation and strategies for effective group work. There are also chapters dealing with more specific issues either in the curriculum or with regard to groups of children. Chapter 7 considers evidence on approaches to teaching reading and Chapters 8 and 9 deal respectively with teaching children with special educational needs and teaching high attaining children.

The eight chapters which consider the evidence about different aspects of teaching emphatically do not add up to a prescription for a single approach to effective teaching. Rather, they present a series of studies which have implications for strategies in particular areas. However, there are some common themes running through them and the strategies which arise from them, while not adding up to a single approach to teaching, have a resonance with one another. Part of the argument to be presented here is that teachers do not typically have to trade-off effectiveness in some areas or for some groups of children against lack of effectiveness elsewhere. The sorts of strategies which can be shown to be effective for, for example, children with learning difficulties or children who have problems learning to read, also have benefits for all children in the class. Similarly, achieving improved levels of academic outcomes is typically associated with improved rather than worsened behavioural or social outcomes.

This book is directed at a number of audiences. First, we want to address primary school teachers who are in the front line of efforts for educational improvement and who, we hope, can make use of the strategies presented here. The book is intended to be useful to all primary school teachers and especially to people on in-service courses and to students on courses of initial teacher education as they start to work in classrooms. Second, we want to address education managers and policy makers at all levels. While the strategies presented here are essentially classroom level approaches, they also need response and discussion at whole school and broader levels. Although the book emphasises the things which are within the control of individual teachers it is not intended to suggest that they are only issues for individual teachers. The approaches suggested here are likely to be most effective when done in co-operation with colleagues, when part of whole-school policies and when appropriately supported and resourced. Third, we want to address our own colleagues in institutions of higher education concerned with teacher education and educational research. It is our contention that in higher education we have paid too little attention to using research evidence on teaching to inform programmes of initial education for new teachers and also paid too little attention in our research to conducting studies which would support the practice of teaching. We wish to draw to the attention of teacher educators the evidence that now exists on effective teaching approaches and to emphasise its relevance for teacher education. We also wish to use the discussions of research evidence which follow to highlight the gaps in carefully established empirical findings about teaching and to encourage educational researchers to see supporting teachers and improving teaching effectiveness as important priorities.

Teachers matter

It is a paradox of much discussion of teaching that it appears to simultaneously celebrate and play down the influence of individual teachers on educational outcomes. The everyday discourse of teachers contains many elements which appear to be strongly predicated on the assumption that teachers differ with regard to their behaviour, attitudes and so on and that such differences have educationally relevant outcomes. The folklore of teaching includes stories of the early years teacher who never failed to have all children reading by the time they left her class. New teachers are told that they will improve with experience. Teacher educators placing students in school are concerned that they should have host teachers who will provide appropriate models. Discussion in staffrooms, in headteacher conferences and at the school gates deals with 'good' and 'effective' and 'committed' teachers, with the clear implication that others must be less good, less effective and less committed.

However, alongside this celebration of teacher efficacy goes a discourse which places the key determinants of educational outcomes outside the control of teachers and of schools more generally. Here, educational outcomes are seen as depending on the characteristics children bring to school with them; either innate characteristics of the children themselves, or factors arising from the circumstances of their families and home environments.

This type of attribution of the causes of educational success and failure can be seen in the large-scale interview survey of primary school teachers conducted by Croll and Moses (1985). The interviewers asked teachers about children identified as having either learning difficulties or behavioural problems in the classroom. In the case of learning difficulties, 71 per cent were described by the teacher as being due to innate, 'within child' factors such as ability or attitude. In a further 30 per cent of cases the child's home and family background was blamed for difficulties with learning. In less than three per cent of cases the teachers identified aspects of the teaching the child received or the school they were in as related to the difficulties with learning. (Teachers could make more than one attribution of causality so these figures do not add to 100 per cent.)

With regard to behavioural problems, within child factors and home and family characteristics again dominated the explanations offered. Within child factors were said to be a reason for 31 per cent of behavioural problems and home and family characteristics for 66 per cent. As with learning difficulties, in less than three per cent of cases did teachers explain behavioural problems in terms of classroom or school factors.

These results are not surprising in view of the considerable emphasis placed in the study of education on the importance of psychological explanations (e.g. intelligence, personality, attitude) and sociological explanations (social class and, more recently, gender and ethnicity). Such explanations are not necessarily wrong and both family background and the individual attributes of particular children are undoubtedly extremely important with regard to educational outcomes. However, explanations which focus on these factors have two major limitations from an educational perspective.

In the first place such explanations are, in the case of particular children, very hard to establish with any confidence. Teachers' knowledge of the personal circumstances of their pupils are often very vague (Abbott, 1996), and, in the case of characteristics such as intelligence, are almost always speculative. In many cases explanations of this sort are essentially circular: a child's poor work is attributed to low ability and the evidence for low ability is the work the child produces; a child's emotional outbursts are attributed to an unhappy home situation as evidenced by the child's behaviour.

Secondly, whatever the truth of attributions of causality involving home and innate characteristics, these are things which teachers and schools can do very little about, and therefore easily take on the characteristics of, at best, excuses and, at worst, negative expectations of how a child can behave or perform. In this book we are concerned to focus on the things that teachers can influence and want to stress that teacher behaviour can improve educational experiences for themselves and for their pupils.

Later in this chapter we shall look in more detail at some of the research which has been conducted relevant to effective teaching. Here we will briefly state the reasons for thinking that, with regard to important educational outcomes, teachers matter.

There is ample evidence that teaching outcomes differ in ways that can be attributed to teacher actions. A substantial body of research evidence now shows that the amount of progress made by individual pupils, *after allowing for their level of initial achievement and background variables such as social class*, differs very considerably between different teaching situations. For example, the study by Neville Bennett and his colleagues at the University of Lancaster comparing different teaching styles found that, across three different curriculum areas, the progress made over one school year by children taught by different groups of teachers varied by an amount equivalent to between three and five months of academic progress (Bennett, 1976). It is important to note that, although this study attracted considerable criticism and the results were later modified (Aitken, Bennett and Hesketh, 1981), these criticisms and the re-analysis of the results in no way affected the initial finding of considerable differences in the progress made by children taught by different teachers.

The ORACLE project at the University of Leicester also found considerable differences in academic outcomes associated with different approaches to teaching. With regard to the progress pupils made in language, reading and mathematics, groups of teachers were associated with different levels of progress and these effects were generally consistent across the different subject areas. Controlling for variables such as the socio-economic characteristics of the pupils, class size and the presence of 11+ examinations made no difference to these differential effects (Galton and Croll, 1980).

More recently, research by Mortimore and his colleagues in London has looked at the relationship between school experience and educational attainment. They found that the school a child attended accounted for nearly a quarter of the variation between children in the rate of their reading progress. Moreover, the most effective schools performed at about 25 per cent above average and the least effective schools at about

20 per cent below average on a series of indicators of academic performance (Mortimore, Sammonds, Stoll, Lewis and Ecob, 1988).

Two further points should be made about the evidence for differential effectiveness in academic outcomes. The first is that the relative influence of socio-economic, school and teacher factors differs considerably between studies focusing on overall level of performance and studies focusing on pupil progress (what is sometimes characterised as 'value added'). The influence of schools and teachers is shown to be much stronger when progress from an initial starting point is the outcome to be studied, while socio-economic factors are stronger with regard to overall levels of performance. Effectiveness, as conceptualised in this book, is essentially about change rather than about a simple snapshot of performance at a particular point in time.

Second, a distinction can be made in principle between the effects of factors operating at school level; types of school organisation, school policies, quality of leadership and so on; and factors operating at classroom and teacher level, such as class organisation and teaching strategies. Although these are potentially interlinked, the picture to emerge from research is that it is the classroom level factors which are the most important and that when these are incorporated into an overall measure of school effects, real differences due to classroom practice can appear to be diluted or unstable over time.

The studies discussed so far have only been presented in terms of academic outcomes but some of them, and in particular the London research, have also considered non-academic outcomes such as self concept, behaviour, attendance and attitude to school. In these areas there were also very considerable differences between the most and least effective schools. Other research on the relationship between teacher behaviour and classroom organisation and the behaviour of pupils has been conducted by Kevin Wheldall (one of the contributors to this volume) and his colleagues (Wheldall and Glynn, 1989; Merrett, 1993). These studies, which will be referred to in more detail in Chapters 3 and 6, show clearly how teachers can make a considerable impact on the behaviour of children in their classes.

The question of the impact of teaching approaches on classroom behaviour raises another important feature of a concern for strategies for effective teaching. We have considered educational outcomes so far principally in terms of the consequences of teaching for children's academic attainment. Another important aspect concerns the nature of the classroom situation and the quality of the classroom experience of both teachers and children.

There is a considerable amount of evidence that many teachers find teaching a stressful experience and that aspects of pupil behaviour are a major feature of teacher stress. The largest scale recent study of teacher experience of classroom problems related to children's behaviour is the research for the Elton Committee on School Discipline (DES, 1989). Two-thirds of the primary school teachers in the study said that inappropriate pupil talk was a daily problem and the same proportion said that pupils preventing others working was a daily problem. A fifth of teachers said that work avoidance by pupils was a daily problem. In a survey of primary teachers by Wheldall and Merrett (1988), over a half said that they spent more time than they should on problems of classroom order and control.

It is worth noting that these are not the major incidents which go to make up headlines but the day-to-day niggle of minor but frequent and persistent difficult behaviour. The work of Kevin Wheldall and his colleagues, discussed elsewhere in this book, has shown how directed interventions by teachers can dramatically reduce the incidence of such problems, while the studies of school and teacher effectiveness have shown how schools and classrooms serving similar catchment areas can differ considerably with regard to them. A recent survey of research evidence in this area concluded that, 'The dominant influence on the classroom motivation and behaviour of a very large majority of pupils appears to be the teacher' (Galloway, 1995, p52).

Educational outcomes

Central to the arguments developed in this book is the claim that the study of education should have a concern with educational outcomes as one of its central features. Implied in this is that educational outcomes should be identifiable. By this we do not mean that they necessarily have to be measured (although they frequently will be) but that a discussion of outcomes should revolve around evidence which can be offered for public scrutiny.

As we said in the introduction to this chapter, we want outcomes to be 'broadly defined' and to encompass a wide range of academic, personal, social and behavioural aims which teachers and others may have as their purposes for schooling. Many of the outcomes with which we are concerned are to do with aspects of academic performance; attainment in reading or mathematics and so on. However, other outcomes may relate to children's behaviour in the classroom and elsewhere or to the amount of time that children spend engaged in curriculum activities or teachers spend on curriculum instruction.

A common distinction made in studies of teaching effectiveness is between 'process' variables and 'product' variables. Processes are educational activities (for example, teacher questions, use of ability groups, pupil task engagement) and products are educational outcomes (for example, reading ages, public examination results or National Curriculum attainment levels). But in many situations it may not be clear whether particular variables should be regarded as a process or a product. In particular, aspects of teacher and pupil activity in classrooms may be regarded as educational processes in the sense that they are ongoing educational activities which may influence outcomes such as achievement. But they may also be regarded as educational products in that they may reflect the aims of teachers and be influenced by other educational processes. In the chapters which follow, in defining outcomes broadly we shall include as relevant educational outcomes variables such as pupil time on-task, motivation, co-operative behaviour and so on, while recognising that for other purposes they may also be treated as processes.

Clearly an approach to effective teaching which takes outcomes as an essential criterion for effectiveness depends on a high degree of commonality in educational purposes. If we are to use evidence on the effectiveness of different teaching approaches with regard to outcomes to inform decisions about teaching then we need agreement that these outcomes are important. We shall argue that there is such a degree of commonality in educational aims arising from the shared professional values of teachers, the common features of primary classrooms as social settings and the external constraints within which teachers work.

Studies of teachers' aims and values concur in showing that teachers virtually all share a commitment to, on the one hand, high standards in the basic skills of literacy and numeracy and, on the other to the personal and social well-being of their pupils. Studies such as those of Bennett (1976) and Ashton et al. (1975) established the centrality of these aims and the more recent work of the PACE research project (Pollard et al., 1994) has shown a continuation of this professional perspective in which a commitment to the centrality of the basic skills goes alongside a belief in the social and affective aims of education rather than conflicting with them. Reinforcing this evidence for largely agreed basic academic aims is the evidence for the similarity in broad curriculum content in primary schools, even before such a similarity was imposed by the National Curriculum. Campbell (1993) summarises a number of studies showing the heavy concentration on the language and number curriculum in British primary schools. The introduction of the National Curriculum has, of course, formalised and made official these agreed curriculum purposes.

Other evidence relating to the problems teachers experience in the classroom show, hardly surprisingly, the high degree of common commitment to classrooms as orderly and purposive work environments. As we noted above, teachers in the large-scale survey for the Elton Report (DES, 1989) and in the surveys conducted by Wheldall and Merrett (1988) had a considerable degree of agreement that pupil activity which avoided work, prevented others working or disrupted the order of the classroom, caused most of their difficulties in school. This agreement on educational purposes, both with regard to attainment and pupil behaviour, provides a context in which evidence for effectiveness with regard to outcomes in these areas will be relevant to all teachers. This relevance does not depend on an identity in the educational aims of teachers but on the existence of shared aims.

Research on teaching

We claimed in the introduction to this chapter that educational researchers have paid too little attention to designing studies directly aimed at improving the processes of teaching. Nevertheless there is a growing body of work which does address such issues and which will be used to inform the substantive chapters which follow. We shall be drawing mainly on research which attempts to link the activities of teaching and schooling to the outcomes of teaching and schooling, 'process–product' studies as discussed in the preceding section. There are two broad kinds of approach to establishing such linkages, each with advantages and limitations, the experimental and the correlational.

In experimental studies the researchers manipulate the educational processes which they want to study in a controlled fashion. They set up teaching and classroom situations differing, as far as possible, only with regard to one variable, the effects of which are being studied. Random allocation of subjects to the teaching situations enables differences in outcomes between different educational settings to be attributed to differences in the variable being studied. In other research designs classrooms may act as their own control groups in 'before and after' studies; other modifications and quasi-experimental designs are also possible. In many real educational settings the random allocation of teachers or pupils to classes is not realistic and, to this extent, the experimental design is weakened.

The great strength of experimental designs is the control of the variables and the random allocation of subjects. The limitation of such studies is that the degree of experimental control needed is often only realistic for a few classes and for a limited period of time. This can mean that only relatively short-term processes can be studied in this way and there may be problems of generalisation to primary classrooms as a whole from studies in a small number of them. However, the replication of experimental results in new settings gives confidence in the generalisability of findings. Many of the experimental results with regard to classroom behaviour and classroom organisation to be discussed in Chapters 3 and 6 have been widely replicated.

In contrast to experimental designs are correlational studies. In these the researchers do not manipulate the settings they study but attempt to find naturally occurring variations in educational practices which are of interest and which can be studied in terms of the relationship of differences in processes in these settings to differences in outcomes. For example, in a well-known example of this kind of research the researchers gathered extensive information about the socio-economic, organisational and pedagogic features of London primary schools and also gathered test data on the academic performance of children in the schools at a number of points in time. It was then possible to see if differences between the schools in the amount of progress children were making in an academic year correlated with differences between the schools with regard to pedagogy, organisation, socio-economic characteristics of their intakes and so on (Mortimore et al., 1988).

Correlational studies can be conducted on a much larger scale and over a much longer period of time than is usual for experiments and their results are therefore more generalisable and often refer to more 'real life' educational outcomes. However, they have the limitation that it is not as straightforward to attribute causality in such studies. There may be problems with the direction of causality and also of knowing if unmeasured (and possibly unknown) features of the naturally occurring settings under study are responsible for any correlations which are established.

The limitation of experimental studies to the relatively small scale and short term arises from limitation of resources and lack of political and educational will to investigate the effectiveness of different teaching approaches rather than from inherent problems with the experimental method. It is possible to conduct large-scale experimental studies as shown by the Tennessee STAR project in the United States; a state funded, experimental study of class size which included over eighty schools and a thousand teachers and was conducted over a three year period. Experimental control of the class size variable and random initial allocation of pupils and teachers to classes meant that the positive effects of smaller classes could be convincingly established from the results in an educationally realistic context (Pate-Bain, Achilles, Boyd-Zaharias and McKenna, 1992).

In the absence of the levels of resourcing and will to conduct such studies, researchers have focused on 'closing the experimental-correlational loop'. If results can be established in small-scale experiments and then similar results arise in large-scale correlational studies, or vice versa, then confidence in the association being both causal and generalisable is increased. Other strategies include repeating experiments in a variety of educational settings and using causal modelling techniques to attempt to test and eliminate competing explanations for patterns of association in correlational studies.

Despite the difficulties in generalisation and attributing causality, many of the results which are now available on the effects of different teaching approaches can be regarded as robust in the sense that they are widely replicated, internally consistent, have generalised to different settings and that different findings have a resonance with one another. A feature of recent research which is highly relevant to our discussion is that, although these studies are often called studies of school effectiveness, the variables which emerge as being most important with regard to variation in outcomes are at the level of the individual classroom (see, for example, Fitzgibbon, 1991). With regard to academic attainment the group of variables which are consistently emerging as central are pupil time for learning, quantity of instruction from the teacher, pressure to achieve and high expectations. The relationship of some of these factors to teaching strategies will be considered in the next section of this chapter.

A final point to be made about research on teaching is that, in common with much research in the social sciences, the results frequently seem disappointing in the sense that correlations or differences between two treatments can seem relatively small. This reflects the imperfection of measurement procedures in the social and educational sciences, but also the very considerable complexity of the phenomena being studied and the wide range of influences on educational processes and educational outcomes. But it is important not to overemphasise the weakness of low correlations or to ignore the real differences which they show. For example, if method A has a success rate of 40 per cent and method B has a success rate of 60 per cent, most people would consider this an important piece of information in making choices between the methods. But statistically the correlation (phi for dichotomous data) between method and outcome is 0.2 and the percentage of variation in outcome explained by method is four per cent. As Gage (1985) points out, major medical and public health decisions are made on the basis of correlations (for example, between drug treatments and outcomes) lower than those which have been established for many educational processes.

Teaching strategies

We have argued that teaching is a thoughtful activity which must be underpinned by knowledge as well as skill. A crucial aspect of this knowledge is a critical awareness of the range of pedagogic possibilities and evidence about their outcomes. Such knowledge constitutes a kind of 'professional literacy' which allows teachers to take a strategic view of classroom decision-making based not only on their own experience but on the widest possible range of evidence.

We are not concerned here with the immediate minute by minute practical skills such as opening a lesson, getting the attention of a class, pitching feedback at the right level or judging when a particular child needs attention. These are important aspects of teaching but we do not, at the moment, have a robust body of evidence relevant to them. We are also not concerned with global features or overall teaching approaches. In the 1960s and 70s researchers were concerned to categorise teachers into broad groupings relating to an overall dimension on which they could be located such as 'progressive–traditional' or 'formal–informal' (for example, Barker Lunn, 1970; Bennett, 1976). These categorisations have proved of limited use in describing teaching, and classroom research has shown that the basic organising dimension does not accord with the reality of actual patterns of practice. Other broad categories such as the teaching styles used in the ORACLE research (e.g. 'group instructors', 'individual monitors') were based on observation of teachers in classrooms but still encompassed widely differing aspects of practice under a single label (Galton, Simon and Croll, 1980). Such global characterisations of practice are of limited use, partly because of the variation in approach within them but also because they do not help teachers with practical decisions about teaching approaches.

The approach to effective teaching which underlies this book deals with what we shall call, *middle range strategies*. By this we mean teaching approaches which are more general than the skills involved in specific teaching actions but which do not attempt to prescribe a global style or approach to teaching. Such strategies are not like the pervasive but woolly idea of 'good primary practice' which has been so influential in British primary schools and teacher education. Unlike this notion they do not serve up a heavily value-laden package of unquestioned orthodoxy. The strategies we are dealing with are based on empirical evidence about the likely consequences of particular aspects of practice and on knowledge about the teaching situations to which they are most applicable. What we are attempting to do is to provide teachers with a repertoire of strategies such as types of seating arrangements, phonological training, co-operative work in groups and so on, which they can draw on flexibly and use in a way that is informed by research evidence on the outcomes associated with them.

This emphasis on strategies linked to outcomes is the context for our argument that teachers should use strategies flexibly. The flexibility meant here is a purposive rather than ad hoc flexibility and involves an awareness of the evidence on the ways in which what teachers do makes a difference in classrooms.

CHAPTER 2

Teacher–Pupil Interaction in the Classroom

Paul Croll

Teaching and interaction

Interaction between teachers and their pupils is fundamental both to the activity of teaching and to the organisation and management of classrooms. As the evidence to be discussed below shows, teachers are interacting with pupils in some way for nearly all the time they are in the classroom. This interaction may be concerned with curriculum instruction, giving directions, hearing reading, giving feedback, holding discussions and social and personal conversations. It is sometimes with the whole class, sometimes with individual children and sometimes with small groups of children. These interactions are central to classroom life and educational purposes both from the teachers' and the pupils' points of view.

From the teacher's perspective his or her interactions are something that have to be *managed* in order to accomplish educational purposes. In particular, they have to be managed in terms of their content, what they are about, and also in terms of their focus, who they are with. Teachers will want to be sure that their interactions reflect their purposes for the curriculum or class management or personal relationships and also that they are appropriately focused in terms of their audience. The management of interaction is an important aspect of the management of the teacher's time which is a crucial resource in the classroom.

In this chapter we shall be concerned with one aspect of the focus of teacher interaction: whether the teacher directs her or his interactions at the whole class, at groups of children or at individuals. This is a good example of what, in the preceding chapter, was referred to as a 'middle range strategy'. We are not concerned with the immediate teaching or interpersonal skills of particular interactions or with an overall approach to teaching. We are concerned with the balance of particular types of interaction and with a strategy for interaction that can inform the immediate decisions teachers must make in the classroom.

In the following sections we shall consider the research evidence on the consequences of the relative use of particular foci of interaction for educational outcomes such as pupil achievement and time on-task. The foci we shall deal with are individual interaction, the situation of a teacher talking or listening on a one-to-one basis with a child; group interactions, the teacher talking to a group of children together; and whole class interaction, the teacher speaking to the entire class or interacting with children in the context of a whole class discussion or similar session. It is important to stress this two way nature of all the interactions we are considering. Just as an individual interaction is likely to involve the teacher listening as well as talking, group and class interactions are not necessarily lecturing but also encompass question and answer sessions, group and whole class discussion and so on.

Many discussions of teaching have emphasised the importance of individualising the teaching process so it can be best matched to the needs of particular children. There is a common-sense rationale for this: children are individuals so they should be taught as individuals. Individualised teaching was given great emphasis by the influential report of the Plowden Committee (DES, 1967). The Plowden Report argued that, '...the blend of individual, group and class work in any one class must be the one that the particular teacher can manage' (DES, 1967, p279). However, there was considerable stress in the Report on the importance of individual differences and the supposed limitations of class teaching. Teaching small groups was seen as a compromise between the ideal of individualised teaching and the practical difficulties this created for teachers. Such difficulties were recognised in the Report which acknowledged that, 'Only seven or eight minutes a day would be available for each child, if all teaching were individual' (p274).

In contrast to this stress on individualised interaction between teachers and pupils is the more recent Department of Education and Science discussion paper, *Curriculum Organisation and Classroom Practice in Primary Schools*, the so-called 'Three Wise Men's' report (Alexander, Rose and Woodhead, 1992). Echoing the Plowden Committee, this Report says that teachers must find an appropriate balance of whole class teaching, group teaching and individual work. But unlike the Plowden Report, which applauded the move towards greater individualisation, the discussion paper emphasises the very limited time any child will receive if teaching is individualised and argues that, 'In many schools the benefits of whole class teaching have been insufficiently exploited' (Alexander, Rose and Woodhead, 1992, Summary).

All these commentators are agreed that teachers must make difficult decisions about how they use the limited time available to them in the classroom and how they can interact most effectively with all of the children in their classes: perhaps thirty or more and seldom fewer than twenty in British primary classrooms. In the discussion below we shall look first at evidence of how teachers have resolved these difficulties in terms of the actual balance of individual, group and class interaction found in classrooms. We shall then go on to consider evidence about the variation in educational outcomes associated with different patterns of interaction.

Interaction patterns in the classroom

A number of research studies have provided evidence on the use of different types of classroom interaction by teachers. The evidence to be discussed here is based on research using systematic observation to provide data on the nature of classroom activities and, in particular, on patterns of teacher–pupil interaction. Systematic observation studies use trained observers to conduct classroom observation according to a very precisely defined set of procedures. Observers have pre-determined sets of categories with which to code the ongoing activities within the classroom and usually employ time-sampling procedures whereby activities are noted at particular timed intervals such as every ten seconds or every thirty seconds. (See Croll, 1986, for an account of systematic observation research methods.)

Systematic observation gives a limited account of classroom activities in the sense that it is necessarily restricted to the observable and to activities which can be classified into pre-determined categories. However, it is a very good way of describing broad patterns of interaction such as whether a teacher is interacting with a single individual, a small group of children or the whole class. Various research studies using these procedures are discussed below and a summary of their results is presented in Table 2.1 (p19). All percentages of types of interaction are presented in terms of proportions of total interaction in order to make figures comparable between studies. This is sometimes different from the way in which the studies were originally reported, where percentages of total class time are given in some cases.

The first study of this kind in the UK was the ORACLE (Observational Research and Classroom Learning Evaluation) study which was conducted in the 1970s (Galton, Simon and Croll, 1980; Galton and Simon, 1980). This research was conducted on junior age (now KS 2) classes and involved a sample of 19 schools in three local education authorities. A particular feature of the research was its longitudinal element which also gave the possibility of a replication study as the same children were observed with a new teacher in the second year of the fieldwork. This meant that 58 classrooms were studied in the first year of the research and a further 40 in the second year.

The ORACLE research demonstrated the overwhelmingly individualised approach of primary teachers in the late 1970s. The teachers observed spent their time in class heavily engaged in interactions with pupils: about four-fifths of the time spent directly interacting. During the first year in which observation was conducted about 70 per cent of this interaction was one-to-one with individual pupils. A further fifth was with the whole class and less than ten per cent was with groups of pupils. Very similar figures were recorded in the second year of observation although the figures for whole class interaction were rather lower and the figures for group interaction rather higher. However, the predominance of individual teacher–pupil interaction was clearly maintained.

A further feature of the ORACLE study was the use of cluster analysis to identify groupings of teachers using similar approaches. These 'teaching styles' contained teachers who, along with other characteristics, had similar patterns of use of different sorts of interaction. These patterns are apparent in the labels the researchers attached to some of the groupings, 'Individual Monitors', 'Class Enquirers' and 'Group Instructors'. However, although two of the clusters were labelled with the terms 'class' or 'group', it should be noted that these teachers spend most of their time interacting with individual pupils even though they make more use of whole class or group interaction than other teachers (Galton, Simon and Croll, 1980).

A second study, published as *One in Five* (Croll and Moses, 1985), also conducted systematic classroom observation as part of research into special educational needs. Observation data on 32 junior age (KS 2) classrooms using a similar observation procedure to that used in the ORACLE study showed the use made by teachers of individual, group and whole class interaction. The results of this study again showed the predominance of individual interactions although not to the same extent as in the ORACLE study. Just over half of teachers' interactions were directed towards individual pupils while just under a third and just under a fifth were directed to whole class and group audiences respectively. The *One in Five* study also gives figures for the range of types of interaction employed by different teachers. No teacher spent as much as half their time in whole class teaching or group teaching while over half spent more than fifty per cent of their time in individual interaction (Croll and Moses, 1988).

A third study to be considered is the extensive research programme carried out in the then Inner London Education Authority by Peter

Mortimore and his colleagues and reported in the book, *School Matters* (Mortimore et al., 1988). This research was carried out in 50 schools in London during the 1980s and included systematic classroom observation, using the same procedures as the ORACLE study. Observations in these schools were conducted in 2nd year junior (Year 4) and 3rd year junior (Year 5) classes and these results are shown separately in Table 2.1. About two-thirds of teacher–pupil interactions were one-to-one with individual pupils while just under a quarter were whole class interactions and about one in ten were interactions with groups of pupils.

The most recent study providing evidence on teachers' use of different patterns of interaction is the PACE (Primary Assessment, Curriculum and Experience) research carried out at the time of the introduction of the National Curriculum in the early 1990s (Pollard et al., 1994). Systematic observation was carried out in nine classrooms of children who were followed for four years during their two years at KS 1 (infant) and first two years of KS 2 (junior). In the analysis presented in Table 2.1, the results from the first two years have been combined to give figures based on observation in the infant or KS 1 classes and figures based on the junior or KS 2 classes. Although each is described as a sample of 18 classes it was the same nine classes of children who were observed throughout although with different teachers so there are observations of a total of 36 different teachers.

The results again show the predominance of individual interactions although the figures are closer to those of the *One in Five* study than to the ORACLE or *School Matters* research. Half of the interactions at KS 1 are with individuals and this increases somewhat at KS 2. For both age groups just under a third are whole class interactions. Group interactions account for under one in five of the total teacher–pupil interactions, decreasing among the older classes.

The summary of these classroom observation studies in Table 2.1 shows clearly that teachers are much more likely to engage in one-to-one interactions with individual pupils than in other sorts of interactions. The percentage of interactions which are of this kind ranges from 72 per cent to 50 per cent. In contrast, whole class interactions range from 32 per cent to 16 per cent and group interactions from 19 per cent to nine per cent. There is some evidence in the Table that there has been something of an increase in the level of whole class interactions across the approximately 15 years separating the studies and a corresponding decrease in individual interactions. There is limited evidence on teachers' self-reports of shifts in the direction of more class teaching which would support such an interpretation (Boydell, 1980; Pollard et al., 1994). The ILEA (*School Matters*) study does not fit this trend but a sample of London schools may not accurately reflect national practice.

Table 2.1: Summary: observational studies of teacher–pupil interaction

	Teacher interacts with:		
	Individuals %	Groups %	Whole class %
ORACLE (Galton and Simon, 1980), *late 1970s*			
(a) 58 Junior classes	72	9	19
(b) 40 Junior classes	69	15	16
One in Five (Croll and Moses, 1985), *early 1980s*			
32 Junior classes	51	18	30
School Matters (Mortimore et al., 1988), *1980s*			
(a) 50 schools, 2nd year junior classes	67	9	23
(b) 50 schools, 3rd year junior classes	63	11	24
PACE (Pollard et al., 1994; Croll, 1996), *early 1990s*			
(a) 18 KS 1 (infant) classes	50	19	32
(b) 18 KS 2 (junior) classes	57	14	30

It is also worth noting that all of these studies show that teachers use groups extensively as a strategy for organising the classroom and, often, the curriculum but that relatively little group interaction takes place. Children sit in groups but the teacher does not typically work with them as groups. Some of the implications of this apparent mis-match between organisational strategies and patterns of interaction are considered in Chapter 3 and some strategies for using groups in more effective ways are discussed in Chapter 4.

In addition to providing evidence on the distribution of the teachers' interactions, the ORACLE study also provided a striking analysis of the consequences of these patterns of interaction for the classroom experience of pupils. In Table 2.2 results from the ORACLE study are reproduced, this time expressed as percentages of time in class rather than as total interactions. The first column in Table 2.2 shows classroom interactions based on observation of teachers and reflects the patterns of interactions discussed above. Teachers spent about four-fifths of their time interacting with pupils and this was mostly on a one-to-one basis: 56 per cent of the teachers' day was spent in individual interaction and less than a quarter of the day was taken up with group and whole class work combined. But the picture of classroom interaction which was revealed when observations are focused on pupils, rather than the teacher, is very different. The second column of Table 2.2 shows the pupils' experience of classroom interaction with their teachers. On average, pupils spent less than a sixth of their time in class in interaction with their teacher and this was predominantly as part of the teacher's class audience. Children spent about two per cent of their time in class (about one minute in every hour) in one-to-one interaction with the teacher and the same proportion of time in a group with which the teacher is interacting.

The contrast between the classroom experience of teachers and children arises, of course, from the necessary asymmetry of interaction patterns in classes which had (in the ORACLE study) an average of twenty-nine children to one teacher. This means that while the teachers' experiences were of virtually constant interaction, mostly on a one-to-one basis, each pupil's experience was of relatively infrequent interaction, mostly as a member of the teacher's class audience. The children observed in the ORACLE study and also in the *One in Five* study (Croll and Moses, 1985) spent most of their time in the classroom on their own in the sense that, although they were mainly seated in groups, they were interacting with neither the teacher nor other pupils.

Table 2.2: Classroom interactions as percentages of time

	Teacher	Pupil
Individual	56	2
Group	8	2
Class	15	12
None	22	84

(Based on Galton, Simon and Croll, 1980)

It is clear from the figures in Table 2.2 that, however much teachers try to increase their individual interaction from its already high level, there can only be a very small impact on any individual child's experience of one-to-one interaction with the teacher.

A further aspect of interaction patterns to arise from some of the research studies discussed above is the relationship between the amount of time teachers are observed to engage in particular sorts of interaction and the amount of time they believe that they spend in different ways. The authors of *School Matters* report that only one-fifth of teachers in the first year of the study and a third in the second year reported that they, '...spent more time on individuals than on either the group or the class' (Mortimore et al., 1988, p80); but the researchers' observations showed that a considerable majority of teachers did so. Similarly, the account of the PACE research shows that teachers reported an increase in whole class teaching over a period in which direct observation showed no such increase.

The mis-match between teacher perceptions and the observational data is not surprising given the pressure of classroom activities on teachers and the difficulties of giving precise estimates of rapidly changing activities. The apparent tendency to overestimate time in whole class interaction may reflect the fact that this is likely to be a more planned feature of interactions and is clearly a teacher-directed one. The consequence may be that teachers are unaware of the extent to which individualised interaction patterns leave children out of touch with the teacher for a very large part of the day.

Outcomes associated with different types of interaction

In the following section we shall be concerned with research evidence on the relationship between the variations in the relative use by teachers of different types of interaction and various educational outcomes. In practice, we shall be concerned with the relationship between educational outcomes and variations in the level of whole class teaching. This is because, as is apparent from the earlier discussion, individualised interaction and whole class interaction make up over 80 per cent, and sometimes over 90 per cent of all interactions so that a higher level of one will almost always mean a lower level of the other. There is less evidence available on the relationship between variations in the level of group teaching and educational outcomes, partly because of the very low level of such teaching occurring naturally in primary schools. A full discussion of the research evidence on effective use of group teaching is given in Chapter 4.

The educational outcomes which will be considered here are mainly those of progress in academic achievement and time on-task. As was argued in Chapter 1, progress or gains in achievement are more relevant for the study of teaching effectiveness than simple measures of attainment at a particular point in time. Time on-task is a relevant educational outcome both because of its association with achievement and as an end in itself with regard to an orderly classroom environment. In addition to these two major outcomes the association of interaction patterns with other characteristics of teacher–pupil interaction, such as cognitive level of interactions will also be considered. These are not strictly speaking outcome variables but they do relate to the educational aims of many teachers and they may help explain some of the patterns of association to be discussed.

Academic achievement

The relationship between types of teacher–pupil interaction and progress in academic achievement will be considered with reference to two large-scale British research studies and also to a summary of the results of many American studies. The ORACLE research project has already been referred to in the context of describing patterns of classroom interaction. It also involved a process–product study of the relationship between different aspects of interaction and pupil progress in academic subjects (Galton and Croll, 1980).

As was shown earlier, the main approach to this analysis was the grouping of teachers by means of cluster analysis into various 'teaching styles' which could then be compared with regard to various educational outcomes. Two styles which contrasted most clearly were the teachers labelled 'Class Enquirers' and the group labelled 'Individual Monitors'. In particular, the Class Enquirers used more than four times as much whole class interaction as the Individual Monitors. A comparison of the progress made by children taught by these teachers showed that in two out of three of the areas tested (mathematics and language) the classes of the Class Enquirers made the most progress of any group of teachers and the classes of the Individual Monitors were among those making the least progress. In the third area tested (reading) there was no difference in progress between the classes of the two teacher types.

These results suggest an association between higher rates of progress and whole class interaction, but they must be qualified in two ways. Although cluster analysis has the strength of being able to identify groups of teachers for comparative purposes, it has the limitation that it combines the effects of all the variables which go into defining the groups. The Class Enquirers and Individual Monitors differed along a number of variables, not just their use of whole class interaction and it is not possible to be sure which variables contributed to the association with different rates of pupil progress. Second, as the authors of the ORACLE reports point out, one other teaching style ('Infrequent Changers'), which did not have particularly high levels of whole class interaction, also achieved above average levels of progress on most of the tests.

A further analysis conducted as part of the ORACLE research correlated the academic progress made by different classes with the levels of different sorts of interaction of their teachers. Unlike the cluster analysis this allows a direct measurement of the association between interactions and progress. However, this analysis is reported in terms of the correlation between the combined categories of whole class and small group interaction and academic progress. The correlation was 0.29 which would normally be regarded as a low to moderate level of association (but see the discussion of strength of correlation in the previous chapter). Unfortunately this result does not disentangle the association with group interaction from that of class interaction but shows a positive association of progress and non-individualised interactions.

The other major British study relevant to achievement and interaction is the ILEA study (Mortimore et al., 1988) also discussed earlier. This study also looked at the association between a variety of school and classroom factors and the academic achievement of pupils. The study found considerable variation between the 50 schools in the study in the progress made by their pupils which was maintained after the effects of various socio-economic factors had been taken into account. The results also showed that the effects of school were consistent for different groups of children; '...schools which are effective are effective for all pupils, irrespective of their backgrounds' (Mortimore et al., 1988, p218).

With regard to types of interaction the study reported that:

> The amount of teacher time spent interacting with the class (rather than with individuals or groups) had a significant positive relationship with progress in a wide range of areas. In contrast, where a very high proportion of the teacher's time was spent communicating with individual pupils, a negative impact was recorded. (Mortimore et al., 1988, p228)

The authors stress that these results relate to the use made by the teacher of interactions with the class as a whole. This was not the same as a teaching approach which simply treated the class as a single unit.

In addition to these British studies a review of a large number of studies in the United States has come to similar conclusions. Brophy and Good (1986) write: 'Students achieve more in classes where they spend most of their time being taught or supervised by their teachers rather than working on their own (or not working at all)' (p361). The studies reviewed are concerned with contrasting teacher interaction with whole classes or groups with situations of heavily individualised instruction. As with the ORACLE correlations discussed above the results combine whole class and group interaction. They conclude that:

> ...they...show positive correlations with achievement for active (whole class or small group) instruction by the teacher and negative correlations for time spent in independent seatwork without continuing teacher supervision. Thus, although these data do not contradict the notion of individualising instruction as a general principle, they do raise doubts about the probable effectiveness of particular programs of individualised instruction in which students are expected to learn mostly on their own....This approach to individualising

instruction does not appear feasible in ordinary classes....(Brophy and Good, 1986, p362)

Time on-task

Time on-task, or the amount of classroom time which pupils spend directly involved in curriculum activities is important to teachers for a number of reasons. First, there is ample evidence that it is related to academic achievement and progress. Although time on-task is certainly not the only factor in attainment it is essential for it. As Karweit (1984) wrote, 'Time is a necessary, but not sufficient, condition for learning' (p33). Karweit's review found correlations between time and learning that ranged from 0.7 to 0.1. The ORACLE study reported a correlation of 0.2 between the percentage of time spent working in a classroom and average academic progress (Galton and Croll, 1980). Reviewing American studies, Brophy and Good (1986) identify the relationship of 'student engaged time' to achievement as one of the 'most consistently replicated findings' (p360).

The second reason why time on-task is important to teachers is that pupil non-engagement in work is one of the main sources of management problems in classrooms. The evidence reviewed in Chapter 6 on the problems teachers most commonly face shows that pupils distracting others from work and engaging in other non-work activities is a major source of classroom management difficulties. When pupils are working, many of the problematic classroom activities are simply not available to them. Doyle (1984) shows how effective teachers facing classroom management problems can use curriculum pressure as a way of establishing order.

The ORACLE study shows that whole class interaction is positively associated with time on-task. The teachers in the Class Enquirers cluster had average levels of pupil work engagement over ten per cent higher than other teachers (Galton and Croll, 1980). More recently, the PACE study also found that, '...classrooms where high levels of class interaction were recorded are also likely to have been coded with high levels of pupil task engagement...' (Pollard et al., 1994, p182).

The most extensive analysis of the relationship between types of interaction and pupil work engagement is that by Croll and Moses (1988) based on the *One in Five* study. Analysis of interaction patterns in 32 second year junior (Year 4) classrooms showed the considerable range of use of individual, group and class interactions by the teachers in these classrooms and also the considerable variation between classrooms in the amount of time children spend task engaged. Relating the amount of time teachers spend in various sorts of interaction and the amount of time their pupils spend on-task shows a very high positive correlation of 0.65 between whole class interactions and time on-task, and a moderate negative correlation between individual interactions and time on-task. The level of group interactions had no association with time on-task. Put another way, the classes of the teachers who used most whole class interactions spent two-thirds of their time in the classroom directly on curriculum tasks, while the classes of the teachers who used least whole class interaction spent less that forty-five per cent of their time directly on task (Croll and Moses, 1988).

A further analysis was conducted of the relationship between levels of whole class interaction and levels of pupil task engagement when children were supposed to be working individually. This showed a high positive correlation of 0.48 between teacher use of whole class interactions and pupil task engagement during individual work. This result is important for two reasons. First, even in the classes where teachers used most whole class interaction, this still occupied less than half of classroom time. Almost all teachers used more individual than whole class interaction and individual work was the predominant classroom experience for all pupils. It is therefore valuable to note that higher levels of whole class interaction were associated with higher levels of task engagement during individual work. The second reason relates to potential differences between the nature of task engagement in different contexts. A pupil sitting listening to the teacher as part of a class audience may be less fully engaged than one working independently on an assignment. The strong association between teacher whole class interaction and individual work engagement shows that the overall correlation with time on-task applies to all sorts of classroom activities and is not just a reflection of less full task engagement during whole class sessions. In classes where teachers spend more time in whole class interaction children are more on-task when they are working on their own as well as in the whole class sessions.

The content of interactions

The discussion so far has considered interaction in terms of the quantity of interactions with different types of audience rather than the nature of the interactions themselves. There is only limited evidence on the content of interactions in different contexts but the ORACLE study provides an analysis in terms of cognitive level. In the ORACLE observation a category of 'higher cognitive level' interactions was constructed. This consisted of teacher questions which sought ideas or solutions rather than factual recall and teacher statements presenting ideas or problems as opposed to statements of fact. Such interactions were relatively infrequent, making up just under ten per cent of all interactions. However they were much more likely to occur in whole class interactions: whole class interactions were more than twice as likely as individual interactions and almost twice as likely as group interactions to be at a higher cognitive level (Galton, Simon and Croll, 1980). A similar finding was reported in a study of science teaching at lower secondary level where it was reported that, '...any imaginative, analytical, thought provoking or enquiry based thinking ...was done by the teacher with the whole class' (Sands, 1991, p767).

The authors of the ORACLE study suggest that the limited time available for any particular pupil during individual interactions and the very brief nature of many of these interactions mean that such interactions are likely to be predominantly managerial and that, in contrast, '...teachers found class activities particularly helpful in promoting more open-ended discussion' (Galton, Simon and Croll, 1980, p138).

Managing interaction in the classroom

As was said in the introductory section of this chapter, teachers must make difficult decisions about the balance of the different sorts of interaction they use. A particular tension is between the instinctive feeling many teachers have that they need to relate to children as individuals and the pressure of numbers which makes whole class interaction a very much more efficient use of a teacher's time. The evidence presented here is that, over the last twenty years in Britain, teachers have resolved this tension by making heavy use of individual interactions, although there is also some reason to think that the heavy reliance on individualisation has reduced somewhat over this period.

However, the evidence discussed here also suggests clearly that a heavy emphasis on individual interactions is associated with less satisfactory educational outcomes than strategies which rely less on individual interaction and put an increased emphasis on whole class and, perhaps, small group, interactions. Major researches in Britain and also in North America have shown that higher levels of whole class interaction are associated with increased academic progress and pupil engagement with their work. The studies have also given some indication of why this should be so. In particular, they show how little time there is for each individual child in a class where teacher–pupil interaction is predominantly individual. There are also indications that one-to-one interactions are often of a mainly managerial character as the teacher re-establishes contact with the child and gives further directions; more stimulating and adventurous educational exchanges are more a feature of whole class sessions than of these individual interactions.

It is important to note that none of these studies provides evidence for 'the more the better' with regard to whole class interaction. In the studies discussed above the high end of whole class interaction is below 50 per cent of class time and the range is between this high of just under 50 per cent to a low of below ten per cent. It is to variation within this range that the correlations and differences found refer and they cannot automatically be extrapolated to higher values.

It should also be noted that although the size of school classes is obviously relevant to the use of effective interaction patterns, the difficulties of effectively individualising all teaching is not simply a function of large classes. The average class sizes in the British studies discussed above ranged from the mid-twenties to just under thirty, and primary school classes currently average within this range. It is clear from the figures presented above that class sizes would need to be very much lower than this average before the constraints imposed by pupil–teacher ratios disappeared. For example, from the ORACLE data used in Table 2.2, in classes averaging 29, pupils spent two per cent of their time in one-to-one interaction with the teacher in heavily individually oriented classes. If these classes had been reduced in size to 20, the amount of individual attention could only have increased to three per cent of a pupil's classroom experience.

Further to this, in all but the very smallest classes, pupils will experience the teacher typically as a class teacher, however much the teacher tries to be an individual teacher. It is in this class audience setting that children get most of their contact with the teacher and access to teacher instruction.

Whole class interaction is not necessarily lecturing by the teacher and need not only involve children in conventional seating arrangements. As Campbell (1991) points out, in many infant classes teachers use 'carpet time' (the children grouped around the teacher sitting on the floor, usually in a carpeted reading corner or similar) for working with the whole class. McNamara and Waugh (1993) have argued that effective whole class interaction by the teacher can make use of a 'horseshoe' or 'square' arrangement of seating. In Chapter 3 of this book Hastings, Schwieso and Wheldall discuss classroom seating and organisation and argue for a flexible seating and organisational pattern adapted to particular purposes as an effective teaching strategy.

The various discussions of classroom practice with which we began this chapter all agreed that teachers needed to find a balance between different types of interaction with the children in their class. The advantage of strategies which result in relatively high levels of class interaction is that they are not incompatible with other strategies. The highest use of whole class approaches discussed here take up less than half of the total time in class, leaving plenty of time for individual and group interactions. In contrast, a heavy emphasis on individualisation necessarily drives out other strategies because, even at the lower end of the ordinary range of class sizes prevailing in British state primary schools, there is still too little time for each child.

The research evidence shows clearly the positive outcomes associated with higher levels of whole class interaction by the teacher, within a range in which it makes up an important but by no means exclusive part of total teaching approaches. It is a middle range strategy which is available to teachers and which can be employed in a flexible way directed at educational processes such as the level and type of teacher–pupil contact and educational outcomes such as achievement and engagement in academic tasks.

CHAPTER 3

A Place for Learning

Nigel Hastings, Josh Schwieso and Kevin Wheldall

Introduction

A classroom is a place for learning, but what sort of environment should it provide? All school architects have faced this question and changes in the solutions they have attempted are not difficult to detect from a casual survey of primary schools. Many of those built in the 1870s, when schooling became compulsory, are still in use today. Their high ceilings, high windows and austere features contrast sharply with schools built in recent decades when the trend has been to arrange for children to be able to see out, to make the space light and to bring the outside inside, with an emphasis on creating a stimulating and open environment. The two styles embody differing assumptions about the nature of teaching and learning in school.

The architecture of a school is essentially fixed: teachers can do little about it. But there are other aspects of the classroom environment which are, to varying degrees, flexible. Features such as the storage, labelling and accessibility of resources, the arrangement of activity areas, the layout of furniture, the provision of a quiet corner and many other aspects of the classroom are all widely accepted as contributing to the effectiveness of primary teaching. Books written for beginning primary teachers typically emphasise the importance of these features and offer advice or prompts for reflection on their use. Dean (1992), for instance, in her highly regarded and widely read book, introduces an eleven page section on the use of space and resources with the claim that 'the classroom environment is a tool for the teacher to use which can affect children' (p193). Because of the almost total absence of research in the area, however, she is unable to ground her advice on classroom organisation in research evidence of its effects on children and learning.

The paucity of research on the educational consequences of different forms of classroom organisation means that prescriptions for practice can be drawn only from argument, belief and personal experience. In this situation, as Alexander (1992) observes, there is a danger that ideas about 'good practice' may become political in nature, defined by those with positional power. There are two aspects of classroom organisation, however, on which research is available and which have recently attracted a good deal of public attention – classroom seating arrangements and class size. We will deal with research on seating in greater detail as this is an aspect of the learning context which teachers can substantially influence. As will be seen class size and seating arrangements may well be related through the ways in which they impinge on children and teachers in school.

Classroom seating

In the Victorian schoolrooms just mentioned, children sat in rows. In many other countries, such as France, rows remain the norm in primary schools (Broadfoot et al., 1993). The move to group seating in English primary schools is generally associated with the Plowden Report of 1967 and seems to have become normal practice by the early seventies (Bealing, 1972). Although no national survey of classroom organisation has been undertaken, an indication of the degree of uniformity can be gained from research primarily concerned with other questions. In the ORACLE project schools (Galton, Simon and Croll, 1980), only 7 per cent of classrooms observed were organised in rows, as were a similar 10 per cent of classes in the Junior School Project (Mortimore et al., 1986). More recently, Alexander (1992) notes that all the classes in his research in Leeds schools had children seated in groups around tables. Group seating arrangements were also the norm in the infant classrooms studied in the PACE project (Pollard et al., 1994).

Current practice is clear: the great majority of primary teachers arrange for their pupils to sit in groups, typically of four to eight. Practice varies a good deal, however, in deciding who sits where. Groups may be formed by teacher allocation or by pupil choice. In the Junior School Project, roughly a quarter of the teachers determined where children sat while a further third involved children in their decisions. Only one in ten allowed children free choice and the remainder varied their methods of allocation. More recently, Wragg (1993) also reports a variety of practice in a smaller sample of 17 teachers: three assigned seating positions, six allowed open choice, at least initially, and the remainder permitted negotiation. Key Stage 1 teachers' responses to questions about their criteria for grouping led Pollard et al. (1994) to infer that the introduction of the National Curriculum may have led teachers to greater use of attainment as a criterion for grouping. 'Sitting with your friends' is always evident to some degree, but it is contingent on appropriate behaviour.

The uniformity of practice in seating children in groups contrasts with the variety of ways in which teachers determine who is to sit where. But, as many have pointed out, the relationship between a 'seating group' and working practice is not straightforward. Tizard et al. (1988), for instance, noted in the infant classes they studied that, 'children are often allowed to choose their own seats in the classroom, so the children in the same group may not necessarily sit together, unless they are working on a joint project' (p36). Groups constructed for curriculum purposes may only come together for briefing, teaching and, occasionally, for tasks which entail collaboration. When the tasks are individual, the 'curriculum group' may be dispersed into other 'seating groups'.

A second recurring theme in commentaries on primary classroom groups has been the mis-match between group seating arrangements and the kinds of task children are given. Although the usual rationale for group seating arrangements is that they facilitate co-operation and collaboration, tasks which require collaboration are relatively rare in British classrooms. (See Chapter 4 and Galton and Williamson (1992) for a review of this evidence.) Studies have repeatedly demonstrated that primary school children spend most of their time in the classroom seated in groups to do their individual work.

The fact that each child has his or her own work to do does not necessarily mean that they should not collaborate, either by working together or by using each other for ideas or information. However, evidence from many of the studies mentioned already shows that work forms only a modest part of children's conversation in this context. Primary teachers seem well aware of this as they consistently identify 'inappropriate talking' as the most frequent troublesome behaviour (Wheldall and Merrett ,1988; DES, 1989; see also Chapter 6).

Sitting children in the clearly social context of a group, giving them individual tasks and telling them to stop talking do appear to be, at best, inconsistent actions. According to Alexander, the explanation for the persistence of the mis-match between the rationale and practice of group seating on the one hand and the predominance of individual task work on the other, lies in the fact that 'the physical arrangement of grouping in primary schools has acquired such a powerful doctrinal status that no other arrangement is even entertained' (1992, p68). He, and his fellow 'wise men', raised the matter again in their influential discussion document. 'All too often there may be a mis-match between the collaborative setting of the group and the individual learning tasks which are given to pupils. The result is that the setting may distract pupils from their work' (Alexander, Rose and Woodhead, 1992, para. 96).

The analysis and the evidence of mis-match are persuasive. So too is the argument that something – task, setting or both – needs to change. Changes in the balance of emphasis between children's engagement in whole class teaching, group work and individual tasks have been both called for and observed, as Paul Croll notes in Chapter 2. There are strong arguments for greater use of co-operative group work, supported by an increasing body of evidence of its effectiveness (see Chapter 4). Alternatively, or additionally, a case could be made for changing the physical and social setting to match the predominant activities of individual task work and whole class teaching. Indeed, following publication of Alexander, Rose and Woodhead's report, McNamara and Waugh (1993) argued for a 'horseshoe' as the best arrangement of furniture to allow for all three modes of working – whole class, group and individual work – but offered no more than anecdotal evidence of its benefits.

There is an obvious danger here of replacing one mode of organisation, established by argument and possibly driven by dogma, with another which is no better supported by evidence of its consequences. Before urging changes in practice, it is vital to ask, firstly, whether different seating arrangements actually *do* make a difference to teaching and learning and, secondly, if they do make a difference, is that difference big enough to be worth bothering about?

Rows and tables for individual tasks

However much the balance of activity moves in the direction of more whole class teaching and more collaborative group work, there will always remain a substantial and important place for individual tasks where children work on their own and it is for this type of activity that group seating arrangements seem so ill suited. Nobody has questioned the appropriateness of sitting in groups for collaborative tasks! To find out whether seating arrangements make a difference for individual task work, a comparison has to be made of outcomes of different seating arrangements. The research task is not straightforward, however. Any study must be designed to ensure that the *only* difference between the experience of the children is the seating arrangement. This could be achieved in entirely artificial and controlled situations, established purely for the purposes of the research, but confidence in generalising the findings to real classrooms would be limited. Consequently, most studies have opted for real classroom settings which have the benefit of being natural but give rise to the problem of ensuring that nothing else is generating differences in outcomes between the classes. One way around this kind of internal validity problem is to compare the performances of the same class under different conditions. In this type of single case, quasi-experimental design, each class works sitting in its usual group seating arrangement (A) for a period and then changes to a different lay out (B) for a similar period and, in many cases, then returns to group seating (A). Performance is then compared across the phases.

The important question is whether children learn more in one seating arrangement than another. To answer it, the *gains* in achievement made in each phase will need to be compared, but this is not an easy research task. First, if a greater gain in one phase is to be confidently attributed only to the differing seating arrangements, then other factors, such as the type of work undertaken and the amount of time available for that work, must be the same in each phase. Also, we would need to be sure that no other work undertaken in a phase could be contributing to the knowledge, skill or understanding that is being assessed. Second, each phase will need to last for a good while for any *difference* in gains between the phases to become evident. However, the longer each phase lasts, the greater are the chances of problems of the first kind arising! Because of these difficulties in comparing learning outcomes, a number of other indicators have been used, 'time on-task' being the most frequently chosen. Time on-task is not the same as learning and it is true to say that we cannot be sure that children are learning just because they are actively engaged with their work. However, learning does require time and children who are spending very little time engaged with their work cannot be learning much through it. Many studies have reported a positive, though by no means perfect, association between time on-task and pupil performance (Brophy and Evertson, 1976; Soar, 1977; Stallings, 1980).

Effects on whole classes

Research on the effects of seating arrangements on children's performance and on teaching has taken place over many years. Wheldall and Glynn (1989) and Merrett (1994) refer to isolated studies undertaken in the 1920s and 30s, but the main body of evidence begins in 1979 with the publication of a study by Axelrod, Hall and Tams in the United States. They examined the on-task rates and disruptive behaviour of a class of 7 to 8 year olds seated in groups and in rows. Average on-task levels were markedly higher and rates of disruption were substantially lower when the class sat in rows rather than around tables in groups. Wheldall et al. (1981) undertook the first British study of this type in two classes of 10 to 11 year olds. In an ABA design, they observed the proportion of time children spent on-task when seated in their usual group arrangement for individual tasks for two weeks. For the next two weeks, the classes sat in rows and, for a final two week phase, moved back to their usual group seating. In both classes, average time on-task was higher in the rows phase.

Wheldall and Lam (1987) undertook a more detailed study in the maths lessons of three classes in a school for children with learning and behaviour difficulties, all taught by the same teacher. Time on-task changed dramatically in each of the two phases when children sat in rows for individual work, rather than in their customary groups. In fact, in each class it roughly doubled. Inspired by this work, Yeomans (1989) undertook a small ABA study in her own mainstream primary school and, with the assistance and co-operation of a colleague, found that the class moved from 49 per cent on-task in the baseline groups phase to 79 per cent when seated in rows. Wheldall and his colleagues have also carried out further, as yet unpublished replication studies, discussed in Wheldall and Glynn (1989). Most recently, Hastings and Schwieso (1995) have reported evidence from two studies involving three primary classes in which precisely the same pattern of findings emerged.

The consistency of the findings across different studies undertaken in different places, in different types of school and over a period of 15 years is striking. In every reported case, children have spent a markedly greater proportion of their time actively engaged with their individual work when seated in rows than in their normal groups. However, as we noted earlier, finding that rows is consistently better than groups in this respect may not be worth paying too much attention to if the difference, though always evident, is small. In order to see clearly the *degree* of difference between average time on-task levels in these two contexts, we have drawn together the results of all reported studies in Table 3.1. Brief details of each study are given, together with the class average time on-task for each of its groups and rows phases.

The scale of the effect of the shift to rows is best reflected by the figures in the final column which shows the difference between mean on-task levels in row and group phases expressed as a percentage of the group phase level. Thus, if a class moved from an average of 50 per cent on-task in groups to 75 per cent in rows, the percentage increase would be 50. Increases range from a modest but worthwhile 16 per cent to 124 per cent, with the ‘average of the averages’, which can only be used as a very rough indicator, showing an impressive 60 per cent increase. This is not a negligible effect.

Two other features of the evidence highlighted in this table are also worthy of comment. Firstly, the largest increases tend to have been made

Table 3.1: Summary of the design and results of observational studies of class average percentage time on-task in groups and rows seating arrangements for individual task work.

Details of research	% time on-task in Groups	% time on-task in Rows	(Average) % increase in time on-task for Rows over Groups
Axelrod, Hall and Tams (1979). Mainstream class. ABAB design; 9, 10, 7 and 7 day phases. Class of 17, 7 to 8 year olds.	62, 63	82, 83	32
Wheldall, Morris, Vaughan and Ng (1981). Two mainstream classes. ABA design; 2 weeks in each phase.			
Class 1: 28, 10 to 11 year olds	72, 73	85	20
Class 2: 25, 10 to 11 year olds.	68, 73	92	30
Wheldall and Lam (1987). Three special school (EBD) classes. ABAB design; 4, 3, 3 and 3 week phases.			
Class 1: 11, 14 to15 year olds	29, 33	72, 67	124
Class 2: 11, 13 to 14 year olds	34, 39	74, 71	99
Class 3: 12, 12 to 13 year olds.	38, 36	73, 70	93
Yeomans (1989). ABA design; 2 weeks in each phase. Mainstream class of 8 to 9 year olds.	49, 38	79	82
Hastings and Schwieso (1995). (A) Two mainstream classes. ABA design; 2 weeks in each phase.			
Class 1: 31, 9 to 11 year olds	56	75, 79	37
Class 2: 31, 9 to 11 year olds.	66, 65	76	16
(B) AB design; 3 weeks in each phase. Mainstream class; 21, 7 to 8 year olds.	48	78	63

by the classes where time on-task in the normal group seating arrangement was lowest: classes that were least on-task gained most. The second and related point is that the variation in on-task levels between classes in the rows column is much less than for groups, with all but three of the figures in the rows column falling within the range 70–79 per cent. Indeed, the lowest figure in the rows column is 69 per cent, which is exceeded by only two of the ten classes in their customary group seating conditions.

All of these studies focused on time on-task, but some also gathered data on other outcomes. Wheldall and Lam recorded levels of disruptive behaviour and teachers' comments and found rates of disruption were three times higher and the frequency of teachers' praise was markedly lower in the group seating phases. Many of these studies have also asked children for their views or noted their spontaneous comments: most found that children strongly favour rows for individual work. Only one published study has attempted directly to measure learning from individual task work in groups and rows. Using the same type of ABA design, Bennett and Blundell (1983) recorded the amount and the quality of work completed by children aged 10 to 11 in reading, maths and language in a school using very structured schemes. Quantity of work was higher in the rows phase but no clear evidence of differences in quality emerged over the two week phases – perhaps for the reasons discussed earlier. Informal comments from teachers in the other studies have frequently mentioned improved quality, however.

Although the evidence looks pretty consistent, concerns are sometimes raised about whether there is a novelty factor at work as the change to rows involves, in almost all cases, a change from the familiar to the unfamiliar. It could be that it is the change to an unfamiliar setting that is responsible rather than a change to rows. If this were true, a change to other unfamiliar arrangements should have the same effect. In one of the studies reported by Hastings and Schwieso (1995), this possibility was checked by examining the effect of moves to rows and groups arrangements on two classes for which normal seating was in a 'maze' arrangement – neither rows nor groups. One class moved into rows first, then to groups and then to rows, while the other went groups to rows to groups. On-task levels were consistently higher in the rows than the groups settings, even though both were novel for these children.

A more frequently raised concern about novelty has to do with the duration of the effect. Moving to rows for individual work may increase time on-task for a few weeks, but will the effect last as children get more accustomed to the set up? Unfortunately there are currently no published studies in which the effects of rows have been monitored for a period longer than about two weeks in each phase, though Wheldall and Glynn (1989) discuss unpublished evidence of effects sustained over much longer periods. We personally know of many teachers who have adapted their practices and continue, after several terms, to find rows better for individual tasks, but, for the moment, well structured, published research evidence of long-term effects is unavailable.

To summarise the position, the evidence is remarkably clear in showing that, for those times when they are expected to be sitting down and getting on with their own work, classes not only spend a higher proportion of their time working when seated in rows than in their customary groups, but that the degree of difference is substantial, particularly for those classes where on-task levels in groups are low.

Effects on individual children

So far, we have been concerned only with the effects of seating arrangements on the average on-task levels of whole classes, but these tell us nothing about the variation within each class. Are all children similarly affected by the changes in seating or is the difference in context more significant for some?

Wheldall et al. (1981) collected data on each child in their two classes and were therefore able to explore this question. Analysis revealed that the children who were most affected by the move to rows were those who were least on-task in the group arrangement. In other words, the children who spent *least* time actively engaged with their work when sitting in groups, gained *most* from the change to a rows arrangement. Children who concentrated well when seated in groups were not much affected by a change to rows. Hastings and Schwieso (1995) report exactly the same pattern. The eight children in each of two classes of thirty-two who were least on-task in groups were dramatically affected by the move to rows. In one class this group moved from an average of 38 per cent of their time on-task in groups to 72 per cent and 78 per cent in each of two, two week periods in rows. In the other class, which spent two phases in groups and one in rows, the figures for this 'low' group were 44 per cent and 46 per cent in groups and 72 per cent in rows. Hastings and Schwieso also reported cases of individuals who moved from on-task levels below 25 per cent in groups to over 90 per cent in rows.

Analysis of the reactions of individual children to different seating arrangements produces the same picture as emerged from the class level findings. Sitting in groups when the task is individual and co-operation is not required makes life difficult – for children and for their teachers. For the most distractible, it makes it very difficult indeed. Sitting in rows gives them in particular a much better chance of learning from this type of task, but it also makes a worthwhile difference for those coping reasonably well sitting in groups. There is no 'trade-off' for the 'pay-off'.

Before moving on to consider the implications of this work on rows and tables settings for individual task work, we should note one final study which, at first sight, appears to show the opposite effect. Rosenfeld, Lambert and Black (1985) investigated the consequences of rows, circles and group seating arrangements for time on-task in some Californian elementary schools. Their results showed that children generally spent more time on-task in circles than in groups, with rows giving rise to the lowest on-task levels. The explanation for this pattern of findings? – the task was brainstorming ideas for writing assignments! Finding that children participate more in class discussions when seated in a class circle or in groups than when sitting in rows will surprise few, yet the related finding that they work better on individual tasks in the less social context of rows still surprises many.

Who sits next to who?

We noted earlier that teachers often determine who will sit where in their classrooms, sometimes using attainment as a basis, but sometimes also gender (Pollard et al., 1994; Wragg, 1993), presumably on the basis that same- and mixed-sex groups work and behave differently. When allowed to choose where they sit, a tendency towards same-sex groups is readily detectable in most primary classrooms and most between-pupil conversation involves children of the same sex (Galton, Simon and Croll, 1980).

In a study of two classes, one of which normally sat around tables and one in double desks, Wheldall and Olds (1987) found that same- and mixed-sex seating arrangements did, indeed, make substantial differences. The first class of 9 to 10 year olds moved from an already high 75 per cent on-task in same-sex groups to 92 per cent in mixed-sex groups. On returning to their usual arrangement, time on-task fell again to 67 per cent. A similar shift was evident in the other class of 10 to 11 year olds who moved from their usual mixed-sex pairs (90 per cent on-task) to having same-sex partners (76 per cent) and back to mixed-sex pairs (89 per cent). In both classes, rates of classroom disruption were recorded and were found to be lower in the mixed-sex settings. Wheldall and Glynn (1989) also report a study undertaken in a secondary school in which mixed-sex seating led to increased quantity of work and, in the teacher's judgement, to improved quality.

The consequences of different seating arrangements and of different seating partners come about for a variety of reasons, some straightforwardly physical in origin and others social. Whether it is the discomfort of being seated next to an opposite-sex classmate that results in greater task engagement, or the fun of chatting with a same-sex mate that leads to less time on-task in this setting, it is clearly children's *experience* of the context rather than any more direct physical features of the setting that mediate the change. In contrast, however, in moving from groups to rows, a new physical environment is produced: fewer eyes can be seen and the context does not facilitate interaction with more than immediate neighbours. There is less to watch and less to listen to: there are simply fewer sources of distraction.

Learning requires attention and children have to learn to manage their attention and to 'filter out' irrelevant happenings if they are to be able to learn in the busy environment of the primary classroom: other children and a teacher can be wonderful learning resources, but they can also inadvertently be distractions when the task is to get on on your own! The extent to which children are distracted is clearly affected by seating arrangements, but it also seems likely that the sheer number of individuals in a classroom may also have consequences for their attention.

Class size and classroom density

Class size has recently attracted a good deal of professional, political and public attention following an upturn in average class size in primary schools and the publication and dissemination of the results of an American study on the effects of small classes in the early years of schooling (see Blatchford and Mortimore (1994) for an accessible summary). The state-funded STAR project in Tennessee is an impressive experiment involving nearly 7,000 kindergarten children taught in 'small' (average 15) or 'regular' classes (average 25) for grades Kindergarten, 1 and 2 (Finn and Achilles, 1990). Assessment at the end of each year has revealed consistently better results for the children taught in small classes, irrespective of ethnicity, gender and school location. A follow-up study is also showing lasting benefits for these children when they have been back in normal sized classes for several years (Nye et al., 1994). Although previous research, generally less well designed and poorly controlled, has not produced clear cut evidence of class size effects, in the STAR project schools, being taught in small classes in the early school years made an appreciable difference to subsequent attainment. This is an important finding but it immediately raises another important question about how this effect comes about. What changes when there are fewer children in a class? Class size effects cannot be just a matter of the number of children in a class. The number of children must have an effect on other classroom processes and activities which themselves bear more directly on learning. The most frequently offered suggestion is that the reduced number results in each child getting more teacher time. It is also likely that teaching methods change, perhaps to include more 'whole class teaching', and that time spent in administration is less. Quality evidence on the effects on process in small classes is lacking.

Children's experience in the classroom when they are not directly engaged with their teacher may also change in small classes. As we have already noted, for each child, the other children in the classroom are part of their environment and the more children in a class, the greater the sources of distraction. But it may not just be a matter of the number of children in a class – the space in which the class operates may be important. The experience of 35 children and their teacher working in a classroom designed to accommodate 28 changes if they move to a larger classroom. Distraction is clearly more likely in the first context than in the second. It may sound like a weak, tautological joke, but there is very little research on the relationship between 'pupil density' (as it is technically known) and attainment, or on the consequences of the experience of being crowded (Weinstein, 1979). Doyle notes that the few studies undertaken on density, mainly in nursery and college contexts, show that greater density 'appears to increase dissatisfaction and aggression and decrease attentiveness' (1986, p402). He also reports a study by Silverstein (1979) in which primary children were more distracted as density increased and that many wanted to be away from those who talked. Similarly, Krantz and Risley (1977) found that the attention kindergarten children paid to their teacher during story time increased substantially when they did not sit too tightly together.

The limited evidence available on the consequences of densely populated teaching spaces is consistent with expectations and with the STAR findings on reduced class size. It also alerts us to the possibility that the beneficial effects on attainment of smaller classes may not be just due to changes in the amount or nature of teacher interaction the children enjoy, but also to reduced crowding. We have yet to learn whether the STAR project database can shed further light on this. In the meantime, attention is better paid to matters over which teachers can have direct influence and on which there is robust evidence.

To change practice?

If the purpose of classroom research is to generate knowledge and understanding that will enable us to improve current practice, what does the evidence considered in this chapter imply for future practice?

A classroom environment is composed of many elements, some of which are fixed and, at least in the short term, immutable. Others are more susceptible to change and therefore available as potential teaching tools. Buildings are at the fixed end of the continuum. Class size, although passionately believed to be of crucial importance for learning, is also not easy to change, although following the STAR results, some schools might choose to have smaller classes in the early years at the expense of years 5 and 6. However, in between the buildings and the displays on the continuum of flexibility lies the organisation of children's work space.

The evidence reviewed in this chapter strongly supports the view that requiring children to sit in groups to undertake individual tasks makes life very difficult for some. Changing the seating arrangement to rows improves time on-task and reduces levels of distraction, with most pronounced benefits for those who normally spend least time engaged with their work. In the light of this evidence, what changes to normal practice would be warranted?

'Everybody back in rows!'

At various times over the last 15 years, sections of the press have focused on this issue and inferred from the research evidence that children should sit in rows and not groups. In the context of a 'Back to Basics' movement, the fact that rows are associated with the 'good old days' and groups with the '1960s' and 'loony lefties' gives added appeal to the inference. To replace groups with rows as the standard form of classroom organisation would, of course, be to miss the point entirely. Rows are as unsatisfactory for collaborative group work as group seating is for individual task work: children should engage in work of both types.

'Group work is a nonsense!'

To our continued amazement, this evidence has also been interpreted as a criticism of group work. It has as much to say about the merits of group work as it does about life hereafter! All the intervention studies referred to have been concerned only with situations in which children have been asked to engage with *individual tasks*, where each has their own work to complete. As it happens, we strongly endorse the view that group work is an area that needs development within primary practice, but the evidence reviewed in this chapter is of no consequence to that view!

'Girls and boys should be seated alternately!'

The evidence from Wheldall and Olds' (1987) study is that, when seated in both groups and in rows, primary school children spent more time on their individual tasks when not seated next to a child of the same sex. The leap from this statement of fact to a prescription, from the *is* to an *ought*, would be large. Time on-task is not the only consideration in making professional judgements. If it were the case that children very much disliked sitting next to children of the opposite sex, for instance, other unwanted consequences might follow from such a change. Conversely, it might be deemed appropriate as a way to increase boy–girl interaction.

'Tables for tasks !'

The minimal justified inference from these findings is that we should think a good deal more carefully than has been customary about how different forms of classroom organisation support the interactions and focuses of attention that different tasks require. This kind of reflection has led a good number of teachers to take up the suggestion first made by Wheldall et al. in 1981 and subsequently by others (Hastings and Schwieso, 1994, 1995; Hastings, 1995), of using seating arrangements more flexibly. Teachers who have done this have developed a variety of approaches to creating a better fit between context and purpose. In schools blessed with a good deal of space, it has been possible to create areas designed for different purposes, often shared between classes. In one school, for instance, a room was set aside as a quiet study room in which children can choose to work and where all talk is forbidden. In another, there are study booths along a wall.

Most schools are too pressed for space to allow choice of seating positions, but flexibility is still possible by moving furniture for different purposes. In classrooms using this approach, the day is planned with classroom layout as one of the considerations and, when necessary, children move the furniture. While group seating may be used for tasks requiring collaboration, 'L' shapes and 'U's, as well as rows, can reduce distractions for individual task work. The children know the two or three layouts and making the changes takes little time and causes little disruption. What time is spent is reckoned by these teachers to be more than compensated for by the quality of learning and work that now takes place – most noticeably by those who did little, progressed least and, in some cases, disrupted the most, when seated in groups for all types of task.

In teaching, as in other professions, there is a responsibility to develop and improve, but to do so on the basis of evidence rather than just opinion about the effects of differing ways of organising learning and teaching. Changing practice is not easy, but we are *not* convinced that primary teachers generally have an ideological commitment to groups. We suspect that groups have just become the orthodox way of doing things and that, as in other areas of life, stepping out of line with normal practice invites attention and possibly criticism. But it can also produce admiration. The evidence of the consequences of a mis-match between classroom organisation and task requirements is sufficient and consistent enough to prompt reflection, to spur movement ('onwards' rather than 'backwards') and to give confidence to innovation in matching seating arrangements to task demands, even if it does mean stepping out of line.

CHAPTER 4

Group Work and Co-operative Learning

Maurice Galton

During the last two decades of primary schooling in the United Kingdom, the patterns of organisation in classrooms have remained remarkably stable. Most children sit around tables (or at groups of desks pushed together). Frequently there are between four and eight children and the groups usually consist of an equal mix of boy and girl pupils. In one study, for example, carried out in small rural schools (the SCENE project) 78 per cent of all observed activity in junior classrooms took place in such groups with a further ten per cent taking place in pairs. However, if instead of looking at the way pupils were seated, the researchers concentrated on how pupils were working, then for only 14.5 per cent of the time that children were seated together were they working together. For over half the observations children worked individually. This pattern of working where children sit together but work on their own has been shown in a number of studies, both here and in the United States, to produce some of the lowest levels of time on-task. The implications of these results for classroom seating were discussed in the previous chapter. Class teaching, on the other hand, produces the highest levels, but in this situation it is the teacher who does most of the talking and the children who listen in silence. After class teaching, however, children working co-operatively in groups produce the next highest levels of task engagement (Galton et al., 1991).

The question of why teachers in the United Kingdom do not make use of collaborative grouping strategies but rather choose an inefficient arrangement (sitting children in groups but working individually) is therefore an important one. In the first part of this chapter, I intend to look at the advantages and disadvantages of group work before going on to consider some of the problems which teachers face when using the strategy and some of the solutions that have been developed to overcome these problems.

Difficulties of working in groups

For many teachers their first experience of co-operative grouping has been that it is more trouble than it is worth. This view has been expressed, for example, by one teacher in Alexander's study of Leeds schools. This teacher said that:

> She had tried to work with one group at a time but children from other groups inevitably approached her and the reception group needed her attention at least at the beginning of every activity she set them. 'I don't see the point of wasting time saying the same thing to five or six different groups when I can say it to one larger group.' (Alexander, Willcocks and Kinder, 1989, pp256–7)

Elsewhere, Cowie and colleagues (1994) have pointed out the difficulties which face teachers, particularly those in inner city schools. They observed a high incidence of bullying, both physical and verbal, which tended to make working in groups unproductive. They noted that many of the studies which support group work have been carried out in suburban schools where there is a much greater level of tolerance. However, Cowie and her colleagues argue that these difficulties are not reasons for abandoning the attempt to develop co-operative learning. They argue that teachers need more help in such circumstances and training in counselling skills. Getting children involved in discussion appears to be particularly difficult. Biott (1987) noted, for example, that, initially, there is very little evidence of thinking in discussion groups. Most of the talk is to do with procedures and children are generally intolerant of each other's views. Biott argues that many teachers, observing the lack of any real achievement in the early stages, therefore, abandon group work altogether. This, in turn, causes pupils to develop low expectations about the effectiveness of working together since the teacher always ends the activity before anything worthwhile has been accomplished. He noted that leadership in groups was often a considerable problem since:

> The official leader did little more than give terms, do the writing or read out the task and children who were expected to be leaders were sometimes bossy and impatient. (Biott, 1987, p10)

However, many of these difficulties are not fundamental weaknesses but arise because, generally, insufficient attention is paid to teaching children to work in groups. This is a conclusion of a review of work in the United States by Cohen (1994) and also by Galton and Williamson (1992) in the UK and in Australia. For example, Galton and Williamson collected the introductions of sixty teachers who were attempting to encourage children to work in groups. In none of these introductions were the purposes of group work explained, nor was the task clearly defined in terms of what children had to do when co-operating together. For the most part teachers concentrated on explaining to pupils what they had to do and what they had to produce. Not surprisingly, once the pupils got into their groups, they spent little time discussing the best ways to proceed and, instead, strove to complete the task as quickly as possible.

The value of co-operation

Those who argue for the use of group work do so for a number of reasons. First, it supplies a supportive and secure learning environment. Second, children can become actively involved in the learning process and third, the relationships between peers and between the teacher will improve as a result of this co-operation. Reid, Forrestal and Cook (1982) summarise this point of view as follows:

> Not only does the small group provide a secure and supportive base from which students can venture out and return as they need, but it also provides a manageable and flexible base from which the teacher can work to provide the best learning experience for the class.

Rowland (1987) endorses this point of view arguing that:

> Without teachers or peers with whom to interact during the processes of learning, children are liable to become entrenched in their present position. This problem arises whether the subject matter is a mathematical investigation which may require new insights or a social enquiry which demands a new perspective on the issue of racism. (p131)

Other views in support of group work have been set out by Biott (1987) who argues that by working co-operatively together the stigma of failure, particularly for slow learning pupils, can be reduced. Furthermore, working in this way, pupils are able to work at their own pace and are less teacher dependent. The children come to respect each other's strengths and weaknesses.

How children learn to think

The main reason, however, for arguing in support of group work has to do with the ways in which children learn to think. Any attempt at planning a curriculum requires some theory of child development which enables a teacher to decide the appropriateness of the content or of a procedure. Piaget's theories have offered an important way for primary teachers to achieve this match. However, over the years, too much emphasis has been placed on the role of the teacher as a facilitator. This has happened because of the importance that Piaget placed on the interaction of the learner with the environment. While part of that environment could be the teacher, Piaget's view of effective learning required that in these interactions the learner should 'self-regulate' the process. In recent years, however, with the opening up to the west of the ideas of the Russian psychologist, Vygotsky, greater emphasis has been placed upon the social as well as the cognitive aspects of learning.

As Wood (1988) points out, Vygotsky's views lead to a very different notion of readiness for learning from that offered by Piaget. In Vygotskian terms, learning depends not only on the state of the child's existing knowledge but also upon 'his capacity to learn with help' (Wood, 1988, p25). In developing his ideas, Vygotsky made use of a key concept which he called the *zone of proximal development* (ZPD). This was defined as the difference between what a child could do independently and what could be done with the support of another individual who was more knowledgeable and skilled. Clearly, the shift through the zone from 'other-regulation' to 'self-regulation' depends on the skill of the more knowledgeable peer in putting new ideas in ways which can be identified by the learner.

We now know that even young children have partial understandings of quite complex concepts. Bennett (1992), for example, tells the story of a teacher with a class of six year olds, asking the question, 'What is a shadow?' Pupils had a variety of explanations. Some thought it was an area blotted out by the sun's rays, whereas others said that it was caused by the body acting as a mirror which reflected the sun's rays on the floor. One child believed the shadow was the little black thing that followed you about! Sometimes, it is very difficult for a teacher to enter into the children's imaginative 'world' and one of the strongest arguments for co-operative group work is that the more knowledgeable peer is closer to the learner's reasoning and can also couch their responses in more easily assimilated language.

More recently, Brown and Palincsar (1986) have attempted to reconcile the apparent differences between Vygotsky and Piaget. They point out that whereas in Vygotsky's framework, learning takes place through social interaction, where in a group, for example, one child will talk to another, so in Piaget's model, the same conversations go on but with the child talking (silently) to himself. In order to make this transition as easy as possible, Brown and Palincsar argue that children need to be provided with a framework or 'scaffolding'. They have attempted, for example, to provide such a scaffolding when pupils are participating in a discussion of a new idea, something Biott (1987) had shown was often very ineffectual. Building on the notion that the acquisition of a concept depends on comparing and contrasting, they set down rules for discussion. These involve first, collecting all similar cases which support the idea and then all cases which oppose the idea. Cases that are 'in-between' are then listed. By reference to these in-between cases (i.e. those that are neither for or against) the group then decide whether the original idea needs to be modified. If the group decide that this is necessary then they go back to the original cases to make certain that they all continue to fit their revised definition.

Thus, for example, in discussing the concept of a mammal, the teacher might provide the children with pictures of mammals, and then another set of pictures of creatures that were not mammals. They would then be given a third set of pictures of creatures which had some characteristics of mammals and some of non-mammals. Brown and Palincsar call this procedure 'reciprocal teaching'. As Cohen (1994) points out, however, there may be some problems with their approach in that the examples quoted generally involve the teacher as the provider of the scaffolding. Thus the sense in which children 'own the process' is unclear, although, presumably, once some children have acquired this systematic approach they can then operate in the group without further teacher support.

How children learn to co-operate

Besides these 'cognitive scaffolds', children also have to be provided with social supports. Brown (1988) points out that there is a 'two-stage process' in learning to work in a group. In the first stage, members have to learn how to submerge their 'personal identity' and to acquire a social one. This happens quite often in schools where children might talk about being in 'blue group' for mathematics, for example. This initial period where children have to acquire this social identity can be a very difficult one. Children either use avoidance strategies to evade participating in the group or adopt more aggressive roles as described by Cowie et al. (1994). The general conclusion of most research on group work is that in order for groups to work well children require social skills training from the start (Cohen, 1994). The pupils must be taught how to listen. They must be taught how to acknowledge an idea. They must be taught how to put across an argument effectively without being strident and 'bossy'. They must learn how to refute another pupil's argument without becoming aggressive.

There is also general agreement that initially, while the social cohesiveness of groups is being developed, more complex tasks requiring abstract reasoning should be avoided. In such situations, if a problem is set which can have a variety of answers, pupils will tend to pick the first answer and stick with it. This reduces the possibilities of participation. For this reason, practical tasks which have a specific solution or problems with only one answer are likely to produce more continuous discussion. Bennett and Dunne (1989) also make a distinction between different kinds of group work. In one kind children co-operate by working on individual tasks but towards a joint outcome. For example, children might be asked to plan a day trip. Some pairs would discuss possible locations, some the mode of transport while others would plan what to do during the day and what they would eat. The whole group would make a joint presentation.

In the second grouping arrangement, children worked, co-operatively, on a single task leading to a joint outcome, such as writing a play. A third group in which children worked individually on the same task was also included as a control. Bennett and Dunne recorded the conversations of the children as either 'action' or 'abstract' talk. Abstract talk, centred on the ability of participants to conduct a genuine argument. In general the evidence suggested that when tasks were structured, so that children had to work together on a joint task, then the level of task-related talk was much higher than in the more usual situations where children sat in groups but worked individually. Overall 88 per cent of the talk in these co-operative groups was on-task compared to 66 per cent in the individualised settings. However, there were also differences in the mode of talk. In mathematics, talk was totally concerned with action in contrast to language work where about 25 per cent were in the abstract mode. This result came about because the tasks chosen for mathematics were mainly practical ones involving manipulation of materials and most of the discussion was associated with demonstrating their use while working through instructions. In language tasks, children were required to evaluate different ideas and the emphasis was on the aspects of creative thought. Talk, in the abstract mode, was often hesitant and relied on the ability of one member of high ability to provide adequate explanations (Webb, 1989). Dunne and Bennett (1990) have provided a series of practical exercises which teachers can use to encourage higher level thinking.

There are also those who argue that an element of reward must be built into the process. Slavin (1986), for example, has developed a number of structures for working in groups around the notion of team games. Every pupil is interdependent in that the total score obtained by the group, for which there is a reward, is the sum of every individual's score in the group. Thus there is an incentive for those more knowledgeable children to teach the less knowledgeable in order to maximise the group's score.

However, Cohen in her review, points out that there is little evidence to suggest that competitive structures of the kind used by Slavin are very useful in developing higher order thinking. In one study that she quotes (Ross, 1988) two groups were compared, one using the team games approach and the other using working individually. No differences in cognitive outcomes were discovered.

We can summarise the main findings of the research as follows:

1. When children sit in groups in a classroom they are likely to achieve more if they are encouraged to co-operate either by working towards a common shared outcome or by making an individual contribution towards a common goal. In the latter case part of the process should include shared decision-making about the planning of these individual contributions and their combined presentation. Such groupings do seem to improve pupils' self-esteem and increase pupil motivation, as evidenced by a greater proportion of task-related conversation within such groups when compared to other forms of classroom organisation.
2. Groups function best when they are of mixed ability but such groups must include pupils from the highest ability group within the class. Where possible it should also be representative of gender and racial differences within the classroom. There is evidence that after training such groups can function well with relatively low support from the teacher. A crucial factor here appears to be the teacher's ability to encourage pupils to assume overall responsibility (ownership) for the activity, thus reducing the dependency upon the teacher for approval of group decisions.
3. Children perform in different ways according to the nature of the task. Levels of conversation appear to be highest when pupils are engaged on 'action' tasks, involving practical activities where they are required either to perform or to make some object or construction. Although levels of conversation will be more sophisticated during more abstract tasks, involving, for example, a debate, such exchanges tend to be intermittent. For this reason some teachers are often reluctant to use group work for this kind of activity, feeling that it fails to generate adequate responses on the part of their pupils. While this observation is true, if judged solely by the interaction, the quality of these intermittent exchanges is often very high indeed.
4. Related to the previous finding is the fact that, initially, problem-solving tasks with a clear testable outcome tend to generate a greater degree of collaboration than more 'open-ended' tasks. The fact that

there is a solution to be aimed for allows children to test out ideas and to reject those which do not satisfy the criteria for a satisfactory solution. With more 'open-ended' problems where the criteria for preferring one solution rather than another is less clear, pupils tend to be satisfied with the first solution offered. In general it appears that pupils do not like challenging each other by debating the value of each other's solutions. They tend to assert rather than to hypothesise or raise questions in this kind of discussion.

5. For successful collaboration to take place pupils need to be taught how to co-operate so that they have a clear idea of what is expected of them. In this process the need for immediate feedback followed by further discussion with the teacher appears crucial.
6. There remains considerable doubt about the value of building in individual rewards within the collaborative exercise so that pupils who perform best receive recognition. One possible way of reconciling the different evidence on this point is to regard group work as a two-stage process, the initial and subsequent encounters requiring the use of different strategies by the teacher.

The above findings offer considerable reassurance to the advocates of group work. It not only appears to be a device to overcoming logistical problems within the modern primary classroom but also appears to offer considerable cognitive benefits for pupils of different ability, gender and race. There remains, however, considerable problems to be solved, largely because the researchers have tended to concentrate on the cognitive aspects of group work and to disregard the social relationships. Although some of the studies reviewed by Cohen (1994) have examined the effect of co-operative grouping on such factors as motivation and pupil self-esteem, this has been done in very general terms and in ways which do not allow the results to be interpreted with any confidence with regard to these important measures. One of the problems encountered by teachers, as Pintrich, Marx and Boyle (1993) argue, is that pupils who have the requisite prior conceptual knowledge 'Do not activate this for many school tasks' (p167). These researchers believe that classroom contextual factors as well as students' motivational beliefs also determine their level of engagement and willingness to persist. Finally, therefore, we turn to this issue, the need for a positive classroom ethos to facilitate effective collaboration.

Creating a classroom ethos for group work

Research has consistently shown that, when problem-solving, a pupil's willingness to activate what he or she already knows is dependent on the strength of belief in their own capability. Social learning theorists, such as Bandura (1986), argue that children gain in 'self-efficacy' by imitation and modelling behaviour which they find acceptable. When such modelling happens unconsciously pupils are favourably surprised by their success and gain in confidence as a result. Much of what pupils find acceptable in the behaviour of others, particularly the teacher, therefore will depend on the nature of the classroom relationships which are developed over time. In considering the nature of these relationships it is essential to recognise that the classroom or the school is not the same as other environments such as the home or playground. Within the classroom a very special set of power relationships operate (Warham, 1993). Observation of ways in which children behave and think within, say, the family structure may, therefore, not be replicated in the school setting when, for example, children are asked to work in groups.

Researchers such as Pollard (1985) and Galton (1989) in the United Kingdom and Doyle (1986) in the United States, have all pointed to the dilemmas involved when seeking to maintain pupils' self-esteem while setting more complex intellectually demanding tasks which teachers often give groups of pupils. When such tasks involve discussion of controversial issues involving, for example, race (Cowie et al., 1994) they usually require learning as 'theory change' to occur, that is they demand that pupils should challenge what they already know. But it follows, since a pupil's 'picture of themselves' is based, in part, on what they already know, that requiring them to question their existing knowledge base carries the risk that the value they attach to this picture of themselves may decrease. The more intellectually demanding the task the more chance there is of perceived failure and the bigger the risk to the pupil's self-esteem. When this happens, as Cowie's study demonstrated, group discussion can soon lead to angry confrontation.

To create a supportive classroom climate which facilitates this process of risk-taking is not an easy task. Galton (1989) has argued that a crucial element in developing this positive climate concerns the strategies used for controlling pupil behaviour. In most classes where children are encouraged to think for themselves the message still seems to be 'when we are concerned with learning I want you to *do as you think* but when we are concerned with behaviour I want you to *do as I say*'. Galton and Williamson (1992) showed, from an analysis of pupils' responses to pictures of classroom incidents of group work, and from follow-up interviews, that children were frequently unable to make sense of this distinction, particularly in its more subtle forms. When discussing in their groups, for example, pupils would be talking and the teacher would praise them for the quality of their ideas. On another occasion, when they were still 'on-task' but 'were not getting anywhere' they would be 'told off' for chatting and wasting time.

Pupils, therefore, appear to see classroom activity as a single entity and do not make the distinctions that teachers would like them to make concerning learning and behaviour. Pupils resent being 'told off' for chatting because they have not completed the group task when, from their perspective, they had overrun the time allowed for discussion because of interest in the topic. When teachers join a group and ask questions, pupils are unsure whether it is to find out what progress has been made or whether it is to find out if they were wasting time. This kind of ambiguity, to which Doyle refers, tends to promote strategies of avoidance. Pupils wait for another member of the group to reply to the teacher to get clues about what is expected in the given context before being willing to participate.

To create a supportive ethos within the groups it is necessary for the teacher to negotiate rules for behaviour as well as learning so that, as far as possible, ambiguity is eliminated. This does not mean teachers giving in to pupils. But it does mean that teachers must be prepared to articulate their needs so that pupils can take these into account when deciding on a course of action while learning how to 'regulate' their own behaviour. For example, teachers do have to explain clearly the reasons why they wish children to work in groups and also their difficulties in knowing whether groups are 'on-task'. Often, however, teachers are reluctant to 'own up' to their problems in such cases lest they lose the respect of the children. For example, rather than admit to their concerns in a situation where too many pupils are talking loudly, a teacher may accuse a group of being too noisy. In such situations, Deci and Chandler (1986, p591) argue that rather than trying to 'con' the pupils into believing that they are doing things, such as tidying up, not for the teacher's sake but for their own good, it is better to 'come clean' and admit 'I feel better when the classroom is neat and tidy'. This approach is just as appropriate when there is excessive noise since there are valid reasons why a high level is unacceptable to the teacher – for example, it is difficult to hear what the other pupils are saying.

Rogers (1990) provides many helpful hints for teachers who wish to move towards this approach and to create positive climates which build up the pupils' self-esteem. This includes a chapter on conflict resolution. He concludes:

> Today, personal dynamics in the classroom are subject to high emotion and fallibility but that only increases the need to plan for the sorts of things you ought to say and do when we discipline. It is possible to develop personal

> school-wide discipline that is more decisive and less reactive without losing that fundamental humanity. That not only makes teaching bearable but even enjoyable. (Rogers, 1990, p276)

This, of course, leads on to a key question, namely why is it that, despite the accounts of the very stressful experiences that many teachers have when managing today's primary classrooms, particularly during group work, there is a marked reluctance to engineer shifts in pedagogy along the lines writers like Rogers suggest? This is particularly true of the inner city schools where the structures which teachers attempt to maintain in the classroom are no longer accepted by pupils who, in many cases, have learned to confront more extreme examples of adult dominance on the streets (Warham, 1993). It is interesting, for example, that in Cowie's account of attempts to develop co-operative learning in multi-ethnic inner city schools, although the teachers attempted to get children to use negotiating skills for dealing with aggression in groups, there are no accounts of teachers rethinking their own behaviour management strategies in similar ways. Changing one's practice in this way may be difficult but, as described by Galton (1989), the rewards can be great. If teachers accept that working together is an important human activity, then learning how to work together in multi-ethnic, mixed ability groups must be an important part of schooling. If, as this chapter has argued, implementing an effective group work strategy demands serious questioning of one's existing classroom practice, then the research suggests that any personal costs involved will be outweighed by the improvements to pupils' confidence and to levels of attainment.

CHAPTER 5
Classroom Motivation

Nigel Hastings

Introduction

Motivation seems to be central to successful teaching and learning. With well motivated teachers and well motivated pupils, few problems would impede leaning in schools – or so we tend to think. Motivation seems to explain why some children engage enthusiastically with their work, some misbehave and others sit quietly and do little; why some persevere in the face of difficulty and others give up as soon as the going gets tough; why some make good progress and others make little or none; why some take care with their work and others seem not to care. Motivation appears to explain so much that is important in schools that it should be a priority concern for educational research.

However, in all of these 'explanations', there is a danger of circularity. If a child's limited progress is accounted for by poor motivation, we might easily infer that the real problem is poor motivation. But, if the only evidence we have of poor motivation is the modest progress made, nothing is gained: we have simply described the same phenomenon in a different way. To be a useful idea, motivation needs to be defined and identified independently of the outcomes it is supposed to give rise to. But, as soon as we begin to push a little at the concept, to inquire about its nature, to debate its sources and consequences and to discuss who has responsibility for pupils' motivation, so the consensus about the central role of motivation in education tends to become eclipsed by uncertainty and confusion about quite what sort of stuff it might be.

As a consequence of difficulties of definition, and in contrast to research on aspects of primary education reviewed in other chapters in this book, research on classroom motivation tends to have been set within distinctive theoretical frameworks. In order to make sense of the research evidence on classroom motivation, some discussion of these ideas is necessary.

Conceptions of motivation

One idea has dominated research on motivation over the last twenty years. Often referred to as *competence*, it has to do with a person's sense of agency, with the feeling of being able to make things happen. The satisfaction and sense of well-being gained from exercising control over a bit of the world can be appreciated even in the very young. A suspended mobile toy tied to a baby's wrist by a length of wool soon results in a fixed gaze and smile as hand movements are followed by the mobile jumping. The child's expressions are difficult to resist interpreting other than as pride in the achievement and a feeling of competence: '*I* did it: *I* can make it happen.'

Feeling able to influence what happens has come to be seen as a vital dimension of psychological well-being in a whole range of contexts (Seligman, 1975, 1991), including the classroom where it has been developed in two broad and closely related sets of ideas. Both start from the proposition that understanding the ways in which children approach classroom tasks requires knowledge of their understandings of themselves and the tasks. The first has to do with the kinds of reasons, known as *attributions*, learners construct to account for their performance and the second with *goals* within the classroom. Adults are often inclined to suppose that the tasks teachers set for children have one, self-evident purpose – learning. From children's point of view, however, classroom life is about much more than this. Learning tasks are just part of a more complex agenda. Before selectively reviewing the research evidence arising from these two views, each needs a little elaboration.

Attributions in the classroom

The study of causal attributions in educational contexts, their causes and consequences, is associated especially with Bernard Weiner (1979, 1985). Attributions to *effort* and to *ability* have been the focus of particular attention because of their central place in the everyday reasoning that performance depends on ability, effort and the difficulty of the task. We should note in passing how this model of everyday thinking completely omits strategy from the equation.

An adaptive motivational style, often referred to as *mastery*, is generally held to be one in which effort is believed to make a difference to outcomes. As effort is something over which people generally think they have some control, the belief that trying makes a difference would appear more likely to result in striving than believing that an outcome is completely independent of effort and due entirely to ability, which is generally treated as being fixed. Believing that effort makes *no* difference is a cardinal feature of a commonly cited maladaptive motivational set. *Learned helplessness* is the attribution of poor performance entirely to factors over which the person feels she or he has no control, for example to ineptitude or to being 'a loser'. A child who has formed a 'helpless' attributional set in relation to reading, say, would apply little effort ('what's the point?') and be largely resigned to failure, to feelings of incompetence and to poor performance providing further evidence of low ability. Helpless feelings may be general, across many aspects of a person's life, or they may be focused in a particular area. In the classroom context, for instance, they may relate to all school learning or to just one type of activity or curriculum area.

Achievement goal orientations in the classroom

The second and most recent conception of motivation to have informed classroom research incorporates many of the ideas within attributional accounts of motivation, but is centrally concerned with children's *achievement goals.* 'An achievement goal concerns the purposes of achievement behaviour' (Ames, 1992a, p261) or, less formally, it is what children think classroom life is about and what they seek to gain from the classroom. A distinction is generally made between two types of goal, variously described as *performance* and *mastery* goals (Ames, 1992a, 1992b), *performance* and *learning* goals (Dweck and Leggett, 1988) and *ego* involvement and *task* involvement (Nicholls, 1979, 1989).

With a *performance/ego goal orientation*, the prime concern is to be viewed as clever compared with others, or at least to avoid looking stupid. Classroom tasks, such as completing worksheets, writing stories, undertaking investigations and answering teachers' questions, are viewed as situations in which comparative assessments which inform judgements of ability will be made. The approach taken to a task, so the argument goes, will therefore depend on how the chances of not looking stupid or, preferably, of eliciting positive ability judgements, can be maximised. A performance/ego goal orientation can be viewed as embodying a 'pathology of the West'; the equation of personal worth with ability, an acute ambivalence about the virtue of effort, the prizing of ability over effort and the consequent belief that it is better to be judged successful as a consequence of ability than of effort.

With a performance/ego focus and confidence in a successful outcome, effort will generally be applied, if occasionally disguised to encourage attributions to ability. Success is not generally the problem, of course. It is when confidence in a successful outcome is low that work avoidance strategies and a distinct lack of effort may be evident. Failing as a consequence of not trying is preferable to risking trying, failing and the likely attribution of the anticipated failure to low ability, the assumption being that if you try hard and still perform badly, you must be stupid! This dynamic has been described by others over the years as self worth protection (Covington and Omelich, 1979; Covington, 1984, 1992).

With a *learning/task orientation*, the aim is to learn, to increase competence. The focus is on progress rather than product, on getting better rather than looking good. 'Put simply, with performance goals, an individual aims to look smart, whereas with learning goals the individual aims at becoming smarter' (Dweck, 1985, p291). Needless to say, learning goals are held to be preferable to performance goals, although Nicholls (1989) argues, with evidence, that these are independent and that it is possible to be both highly ego and task oriented. The general tendency of much of the literature is to imply that a competitive, performance/ego orientation is educationally less satisfactory, both intrinsically and for affective and cognitive outcomes, than a learning/task goal orientation.

However, the difference between these two orientations is not just a matter of goal as, according to Dweck (1991), they embody two importantly different understandings of 'ability'. Associated with an ego/performance orientation is a view of ability as a fixed 'entity', as is assumed in much of the research on attributions. In contrast, Dweck suggests, with a learning goal orientation there is both a belief that effort pays off and an associated conception of ability as not being static and fixed, but as being susceptible to longer-term development through the application of effort. With a task/learning orientation, failures are not all bad news: they are a necessary part of learning and contribute both to improving performance and to becoming 'cleverer'.

Research on motivation in the primary classroom

Before beginning to consider the research evidence on motivation in the classroom, there are a number of surprising and, from our point of view, disappointing aspects of the now very substantial body of research that are worth highlighting. First, British readers may be discomforted to know that almost no research has been undertaken in the UK while in other parts of Europe, in Australia, New Zealand and especially in the USA, motivation has been a very active research area. Second, relatively few studies have involved children in the primary school age range and been conducted in school settings. Extrapolation from studies of older students or from contrived situations necessarily warrants caution. Lastly, although motivation attracts most attention in teaching when it is felt to be lacking, only a limited amount of research energy has so far been directed at identifying and evaluating strategies for enhancing motivation in the classroom.

Having noted these points, we will consider the evidence through three broad and related questions: 'Does motivation matter?', 'Do classroom processes relate to children's perceptions?' and 'How can motivation be enhanced in the classroom?'

Does motivation matter?

At face value, this is a silly question. Any definition of motivation in education which did not entail a logical connection with progress would be self-evidently absurd. The question is not absurd, however, when applied to operational definitions of motivation. Research on motivation has drawn on the essential idea that it is the perception of self, task and situation which inform the approach which is taken. In this context, it is sensible to ask whether primary school children actually *do* formulate understandings of the kinds suggested by attribution and goal theory and whether children forming differing perceptions differ in other respects, particularly in relation to educational outcomes.

One of the paradoxes of an approach which is concerned with learners' explanations for their progress and performance, is the scarcity of research allowing children to express their attributions in their own words. Much of the research has required them to choose from a provided list of causes (e.g. ability, effort, luck and task difficulty). An exception is a study by Little (1985) in which children in the 5 to 14 age range were asked to account for a number of classroom situations; to explain, for example, why a child in their class whom they have identified as 'working well', is doing so. Children's responses involved fairly frequent reference to ideas about effort and ability, as well as other types of attribution, notably to behaviour ('he doesn't muck about'). In a partial replication, Rogers (1990) produced similar results. Both studies also identified age-related changes in children's attributions which raise a number of issues, not least of which is their understanding of ideas like 'ability' and 'effort'. Indeed, in Little's study, the ways in which children talked suggested a lack of differentiation between performance and ability.

Children's understandings of classroom life are necessarily constructed within the concepts they have available. Developmental studies suggest that it is not until the middle years of primary education that most come to differentiate the key concepts of ability, effort and task difficulty and begin to use them in ways which parallel adults' usage (Nicholls, 1983, 1984, 1989). It is not unusual to hear a five year old explain, particularly following teacher praise, that she did well at a task 'because' she is good at maths, tried hard *and* that the work was easy! The three concepts are poorly differentiated, leading all the 'good' qualities to be packaged together.

This lack of differentiation has led some commentators to suggest that children in the early primary years are not prone to disabling motivational beliefs as they all seem to think that everyone can do well if they try hard, and also that if they do well they must have high ability and have tried hard. The evidence is a little confusing, however. Licht (1992) discusses a number of studies reporting no decrease in persistence following failure by children below about eight years of age, while Dweck (1991) reports others in which pre-school and young school children show helpless behaviours and beliefs. It does appear, however, that young children are less prone to developing disabling beliefs than those aged about seven or more who are beginning to develop a normative conception of ability. As we shall see, this may not just be a developmental trend but also a consequence of the ways in which nursery and infant classes operate and the experience of some individual children may lead to disabling beliefs, and to helplessness in particular, from a younger age.

Studies identifying young children's goal orientations are limited. However, a number of British studies in which children's understandings and criteria of preference for classroom tasks have been elicited are relevant. Bennett et al. (1984) noted children's lack of awareness of the learning purposes that lay behind the tasks their teachers asked them to engage in and the ways in which their attention focused on the form of their work. In the PACE project, children were also asked why they thought their teachers wanted them to do particular tasks. About a quarter of 5 to 7 year olds' answers reflected a general understanding that learning was the purpose, increasing from Year 1 to Year 2. A similar proportion simply indicated that the work was 'required' and 13 per cent of responses were coded as 'Don't know' (Pollard et al., 1994). When in Year 3 and Year 4 these same children indicated an increased preference for easy, structured activities which provide a high chance of success (Pollard, 1996). They also continued to show an encouraging preference for 'effort' over 'ability' in their explanations of classroom achievement, although the evidence previously mentioned suggests that this will change before the end of primary school (Nicholls, 1983, 1984, 1989).

It is clear that children in the primary years do engage in reasoning about themselves, tasks and outcomes, at least when they are asked about them, and that marked developmental changes take place in their understanding and use of some motivationally relevant concepts. We can therefore turn now to ask whether differences in educational outcomes are associated with different attributions and goals.

Children's perceptions, learning and attainment

Studies exploring links between children's attributions or goal orientations and attainment in school are limited in number and varied in their findings. Meece and Holt (1993), for instance, report associations between goal orientations and attainment in science and other subjects for 11 to 12 year olds, with those high in task orientation alone achieving better grades than those who were high in both task and ego orientation. In line with attribution theory, studies reviewed by Licht (1992) indicate that lower attaining children are more likely than others to attribute poor performance to low ability. Also, Nicholls (1979) reports an increasing association in children aged 6 to 12 between ratings of themselves as readers and attributions of reading skill to ability rather than effort. However, no links were found between maths attainment and either self-efficacy, the belief that you 'have what it takes', among 9 to 10 year olds (Norwich, 1987), or goal orientation in 8 to 12 year olds (Yates, Yates and Lippett, 1995), though a link with a measure of helplessness was identified.

It is apparent that the link between attributions or goal orientations and attainment is not straightforward, but nor is it likely to be: children of similar attainment vary substantially in confidence. A closer relationship might be expected between children's perceptions and the progress they make, but no research of this kind has yet been undertaken using an attributional or goal orientation framework. The ORACLE project employed a questionnaire concerned with aspects of motivation and anxiety but revealed no clear relationships with learning (Croll and Willcocks, 1980).

Many aspects of 'approach to study' have been found to relate to perceptions. Ames (1992a) and Jagacinski (1992) provide useful summaries of research indicating relationships between task orientation and time spent on tasks, persistence in the face of difficulty, self-monitoring, variety of learning strategies used and a number of other qualities which are likely to support learning. A marked performance/ego orientation, meanwhile, tends to be associated with work avoidance and use of short-term, superficial strategies like rote learning when success is not anticipated. However, the great majority of these studies are not conducted with children in the primary age range, about whom relatively little is known in these terms.

Children's perceptions and behaviour

As we have noted in other chapters, attainment is not the only important outcome of education: behaviour is another. Research on classroom behaviour is reviewed in Chapter 6, but it also relates to motivation as children whose behaviour causes concern in class are often also considered by their teachers to be poorly motivated. Fry and Grover (1984, see also Fry, 1987) studied children aged 6, 8 and 10 identified by their teachers as 'problem' or 'non-problem' children. Matched for attainment level, the two groups were asked to account for the performance of children in a number of stories. For both success and failure, the problem children were much more inclined to attribute the outcome to factors over which the child in the story had no control, such as mood, luck or the difficulty of the task, with this tendency becoming more pronounced with age. Assuming some degree of identification with the stories, these children saw little relation between their actions and outcomes: success and failure seem to them to 'happen'.

The evidence of possible links between children's perceptions in classroom learning contexts and educational outcomes, though not strong, is sufficient to indicate that these should be considered as potentially important for progress and performance. However, it is not just the potential role of these beliefs in attainment that makes them significant. Like good behaviour, a mastery/task orientation and feelings of agency and competence can be considered both as important for classroom learning and as desirable educational outcomes in themselves.

Do classroom processes relate to children's perceptions?

If these perceptions are important, how do they come about? Attributions and goal orientations develop as a consequence of experience. Consistent experience of success, for instance, will lead to attributions of high ability just as an unleavened diet of failure will give rise to a low ability judgement. However, attributions and orientations are also affected by the specifics of situations as well as by consistencies between them. If research in this area is to be useful to primary teachers, it must identify features of classroom practice which serve to support the development of both adaptive and maladaptive goal orientations. The American researcher Carole Ames (1992a, 1992b) has been particularly concerned with identifying features of classroom teaching which support the development of mastery/task orientations in primary schools. She has drawn on the earlier work of Epstein (1989) who used six headings, giving the acronym TARGET, to organise evidence and ideas. We will do the same.

Tasks

Evidence that children work in a manner consistent with a mastery orientation when tasks are varied, experienced as interesting and perceived as being purposeful and within their competence to complete will surprise few. The perceived pointlessness of some classroom tasks and primary children's frequent lack of appreciation of their learning purposes, may be remedied by explaining the rationale. Although this is clearly no master key to the vault of interest, teachers rarely make the learning purposes of tasks explicit when giving instructions but focus on the requirements of the product that is to emerge, a tendency which would appear more likely to support an ego than a task orientation.

Children's willingness to apply effort, their beliefs about the effectiveness of effort and their learning benefit from the use of clear and specific *goal setting*, particularly if children themselves set the goals (Schunk, 1983a, 1985). Clear goals provide a structure within which to experience progress. The greater degree of structure inherent in some curriculum subjects may fulfil the same purpose of supporting a focus on progress and learning and of fostering a task orientation. A recent study undertaken at Lancaster University found children in their final year at primary school more inclined to mastery, defined by their response to failure, for mathematics than for English (Rogers et al., 1994; Rogers, 1994). The experience of structure appears significant in supporting a focus on learning when confidence is not strong as progress is more easy to determine where a structure is evident. The increasing preference for structured tasks expressed by children moving into Years 3 and 4 has already been noted (Pollard, 1996).

Authority

Within the TARGET framework, authority refers to the extent to which children experience a degree of control over their own activities and learning, the plausible assumption being that a mastery/task goal orientation necessitates a degree of self-direction and autonomy. Grolnick and Ryan (1987) and Ames (1992a, 1992b) review a series of studies reporting links between children's experience of autonomy and support within their classrooms and the development of beliefs and behaviours associated with a task orientation.

The areas of classroom life in which it is appropriate for teachers to support the development of autonomy are substantial but also bounded. Evidence from the PACE studies indicates children's experience of teacher determination of tasks increases, particularly from Year 1 to Year 2, although there were no indications that children thought this inappropriate (Pollard, 1996). However, choice of task is not the only dimension in which children can exercise control. The organisation and management of work, choice of strategy and evaluation are all matters in which control can move between teacher and child and be negotiated. The Junior School Project (Mortimore et al., 1988) found that where teachers provided a structure in which children had accountable responsibility for managing their own work over a *limited* period of time, the impact was positive on a number of outcomes. Responsibility extending over longer periods, a day or more, was associated with poorer outcomes.

Recognition

The TARGET area of recognition refers to the ways in which and circumstances under which teachers use rewards and praise in the classroom. If these are used in an essentially competitive context, where receipt is contingent on performing better than others, their use is clearly likely to foster a performance/ego orientation to the double disadvantage of those who do not receive them. By the same reasoning, praise and rewards which are used to acknowledge progress rather than level of achievement are likely to support a task orientation by indicating that it is learning that is important, and evidence suggests that this is the case (Schunk, 1983b).

Some studies have indicated that extrinsic rewards can undermine intrinsic motivation and task orientation, but a recent meta-analysis of 96 experimental studies shows that this only happens where rewards are given simply for engaging with a task, no matter how well (Cameron and Pierce, 1994). Indeed, the analysis suggests verbal praise has positive effects on intrinsic motivation.

Praise can have unintended motivational consequences if it is not used skilfully, however. The developmental changes in children's understanding of effort and ability discussed earlier, have ramifications for the ways in which they interpret teachers' comments. At all ages, children understand that teachers praise effort, but older primary children tend to judge a child who receives praise for unremarkable achiev ment as having low ability. Similarly, and again assuming a normative evaluative framework, they come to understand criticism for failure at a hard task as a high ability cue (Barker and Graham, 1987; Butler, 1994). The important point to note is that the reasons for both praise and criticism should be made explicit if they are to support motivationally fruitful attributions. Fuller discussions of this point are provided by Brophy (1981) and Schwieso and Hastings (1987).

Grouping

Collaborative group work, in which children not only undertake a task together but also determine how it is to be undertaken, also supports autonomy and the development of a task orientation (Nicholls et al., 1990), although group work strategies such as those advocated by Slavin (1990) which involve collaboration within and competition between groups, could serve to support both goal orientations. However, the emerging evidence on group work indicates that it *can* support the independence and high levels of involvement. If not well prepared for, however, the open-ended nature of many group work tasks can give rise to uncertainty and work avoidance, perhaps especially where children are accustomed to a strong performance/ego focus (see Chapter 4). Peer tutoring also involves collaboration between children, provides both structure and responsibility and has well established beneficial outcomes, particularly for reading. Topping (1987, 1988, 1992) and Wheldall and Glynn (1989) provide useful reviews.

Evaluation

Evaluation is implicit in many of the TARGET areas and plays a crucial role in informing classroom goal orientations. Through their comments and actions, teachers distinguish the worthwhile from the less worthwhile and inform children's understanding of success. Where evaluation is normative, involving comparisons and therefore competition between pupils, where success is about being the best, a performance/ego orientation is fostered, but where evaluation relates to change and involves comparison with previous performance, attention is directed to progress and learning. The evidence is that these differing approaches have their predicted effects on children's goal orientations and attributions (Ames, 1984; Nicholls, 1989).

Evaluative criteria are not in evidence only at the completion of a task, however. The way in which a task is introduced can indicate, or allow inferences about, its purpose and the criteria for evaluation. Instructions designed to induce competition and ego-involvement have been demonstrated to influence children's approach in predictable ways, depending on their estimation of how well they will do (Jagacinski, 1992).

Time

Time is the final TARGET area and it is central to most of the others. Learning and progress entail change over time; classroom learning, tasks and goals are set within clear time structures; and time features in teachers' assessments of children's performance and progress. Perhaps most importantly from a motivational perspective, however, the experience of competence and agency requires attention to the relationships between events within time. Indeed a feature of some children who seem to 'lack motivation' in the classroom is the way they appear to experience no time structure bounding their engagement with classroom tasks.

In summary, theory and research evidence support the proposition that classroom processes, helpfully considered under the TARGET areas, influence the overall motivational climate of classrooms. Moreover, although the research evidence so far falls short of being robust, features of classroom practice which serve to support motivation for learning are beginning to emerge and warrant at least reflective attention.

How can motivation be enhanced in the classroom?

Getting children to do the things that they want to do has never been a teacher's concern. However, as Brophy (1987) points out, teachers are more like 'work supervisors' than 'recreation program directors' (p41) and have to find ways to motivate children to engage with tasks which they do not always immediately, or possibly ever, find intrinsically interesting. There is therefore a reasonable concern that research should inform the development and evaluation of strategies to enhance motivation. The TARGET framework helps to highlight some of the dimensions of classroom process which have a bearing on the development of motivationally relevant perspectives and understandings, but evidence on specific classroom strategies to enhance motivation could yet be more useful.

Ames suggests that 'enhancing motivation means enhancing children's valuing of effort and a commitment to effort-based strategies through the design of mastery-oriented structures' (1992a, p268), but the professional responsibilities of teachers require that enhancing motivation should do more than change children's beliefs. It must also increase engagement with classroom tasks and lead to improvements in progress and achievement.

Children have their own ideas about what teachers could do to increase their motivation, of course. Young primary age children thought all of the twelve possible teacher strategies Nolen and Nicholls (1993) suggested to them would help them learn more maths, though they were least impressed with the idea of being able to choose their own work. Eleven year olds were more discerning and favoured 'increased interest' and 'co-operative learning' while expressing little enthusiasm for being praised. However, a subsequent study suggests that 7 to 12 year olds' ideas about effective and fair strategies relate more to their ideas about the purposes of education than to their age (Thorkildsen, Nolen and Fournier, 1994). Whether the strategies children think would be motivating for them would be in practice is, of course, a different question.

A number of research-informed lists of strategies for enhancing classroom motivation have been developed. Brophy (1987) offers a 'starter set' of 33, while Alderman (1990) suggests just four 'Links' for working with helpless students. A more recent book by Raffini (1993), however, offers a full 50 'field tested' strategies, classified by TARGET area and grade level. Useful though these may prove to be, very few classroom strategies for enhancing the motivation for learning of individual children have been the subject of systematic evaluation. Two are worthy of particular mention, however.

Attribution retraining

If children's perceptions are central to their motivation for classroom learning, one approach to enhancing motivation would be to teach children with disabling attributional tendencies to change their interpretations of their experiences and to construe things differently. Craske (1985) used attribution retraining for failure with children who reduced effort after failure but, finding it more successful with girls than with boys, reasoned that some of the boys were not helpless but had avoided trying in order to preserve their self worth. In a further study, she found that attribution retraining was successful with children displaying helpless characteristics, but was unsuccessful with children who appeared to avoid effort in order to protect against low ability attributions and defend their feelings of self worth (Craske, 1988). As we noted earlier, for performance/ego oriented, unsuccessful children, effort is 'a double-edged sword' and encouragement to apply effort is useless. Thompson (1994) has recently suggested that the problem with self worth preservers is not the way they view failures, but the fact that they do not feel they caused their successes. Attribution retraining should therefore focus on leading such children to attribute successful outcomes internally, to their own skill, effort and ability, he suggests.

The limited work on attribution retraining with primary school children is encouraging. It highlights the potential role of teachers in fostering attributions to effort for both successful and unsuccessful outcomes. For successful outcomes, attributions to both effort and *increasing* ability promote a greater sense of competence and more focused application of effort.

The attunement strategy

To be of use in the context of everyday classroom teaching, strategies to enhance motivation must not only be effective, they must require little of a class teacher's time.

The *Attunement Strategy* has been developed with this practical requirement in mind by Stevens, Van Werkhoven and their colleagues in Utrecht who have developed a training programme designed to furnish Dutch primary school staff teams with the skills and knowledge to use the strategy (Castelijns et al., 1992).

Children for whom the approach is most appropriate are those judged by their teachers to be underachieving. They may spend excessive amounts of time involved in procedures such as sharpening pencils, queuing but never getting to the front, arranging their resources, writing little and rubbing out most of it. Many tend to be inattentive and either passive participants or non-participants in classroom activities, a pattern of behaviour which a recent large-scale American study suggests should be the target for early intervention to forestall the development of increasing educational difficulties (Finn and Cox, 1992; Finn, Pannozzo and Voelkl, 1995). Rather than necessarily giving themselves disabling attributions, it is suggested that many of these children may have given up even reacting differentially to tasks, as if they believe that 'Work is stuff that comes along, hangs about for a while and then goes away as some more arrives – no matter what I do'. Whatever their beliefs, such children are certainly not learning or mastery oriented.

With underachieving children such as these, a common approach is to take care to give very explicit instructions about what is to be done and how, by setting time and quality or quantity goals and sub-goals, for example. Once some progress has been made, praise and other intended reinforcers would be given as well as informational feedback about the work completed. This type of approach often bears fruit, but it is characterised by a high degree of teacher control. It does not take the pupil's perspective into account and, so the argument goes, may do little to foster internal attributions for success. Consequently, change can be highly context specific and prone to rapid fading.

The Attunement Strategy involves the teacher in changing the way in which she or he introduces a task to the target child and the way feedback is given. The intervention involves brief conversations concerning task definition, method, goal setting and, when underway or completed, outcomes – but with a difference. Rather than take complete control, the teacher tries to get the child to define the task, to specify the outcomes and, subsequently, to assess the work. In addition, however, the pupil is prompted to consider aspects such as how hard the task is likely to be, whether she or he will need to try hard, whether it will be interesting and, on completion, to review those predictions.

The purpose of the pre-task discussion is to involve the child in anticipating, estimating, planning and goal setting. So, in one conversation, a teacher might enquire, 'Well, what do you think of this one, does it look hard?'...'What do you think you will need to make that?'...'How far do you think you will get by lunchtime?' On another occasion, discussion might focus more on setting quality goals, or on anticipating points at which help might be needed. Each conversation lasts no more than a couple of minutes before the child is left to work. The purpose of the conversation is to prompt the forming of explicit predictions about the experience and about likely outcomes. Any tendency by the child to set unreasonably ambitious goals should be moderated!

Once work is underway, or on completion, rather than the teacher leaping in with plentiful praise, the strategy entails a further conversation in which the anticipated experience is compared with the actual. 'So, was it as hard as you thought it was going to be?'...'Did you need the big scissors?'...'You said you thought it looked boring, was it?'...'OK, it's lunchtime! How far did you get?'

On occasions, quality discussions will be appropriate. The point is not that teachers should hand over all evaluative responsibilities to the children, merely that they should prompt children to engage in reflection and evaluation, drawing attention particularly to improvement and progress. A final important element is discussion about how successes have been achieved. 'So how come you got this all done 15 minutes before lunchtime?' The intention here, of course, is to stimulate attributions to internal factors such as effort and increasing competence and to foster a sense of agency and competence.

The Attunement Strategy is not a set routine but a highly skilful interaction. All 'motivational attempts can be overdone, and any particular strategy can lose its effectiveness if it is used too often or too routinely' (Brophy, 1987, p42) and the Attunement Strategy is no exception. However, evidence of its value is accumulating. Van Werkhoven and Stevens (in press) report on its fruitful use in 14 classes of 8 to 11 year olds in the Netherlands and evidence of marked gains in task engagement emerged in pilot programmes in primary classrooms in the UK and Germany (van Werkhoven, in press). Less formal evidence on teachers' use of the strategy is also available (Doran and Cameron, 1995; Hastings, 1992, 1994). Additionally, currently unpublished observational data from the classrooms of 12 primary teachers employing the strategy in the context of an in-service programme shows a change in the mean times on-task of their chosen pupils from 35 per cent to 55 per cent over a period of three weeks. However, as many teachers have commented, it is the change in body posture and movement as a sense of competence begins to flow that is more rewarding to observe (Hastings, in preparation).

While the TARGET framework is helpful for considering the ways in which classroom processes as a whole contribute to the formation of adaptive educational goal orientations at the whole class level, evidence and experience of the Attunement Strategy, which embodies many of the research-informed ideas in the TARGET areas, indicates that it is a practicable and fruitful way of enhancing the motivation of individual children in the classroom. There is, however, a need for further research to evaluate the approach in a wider range of contexts and to determine its appropriateness for children with differing types of attributional patterns and goal orientations.

Concluding comments

Educators have generally valued intrinsic motivation but prescriptions about what to do in its absence have often been little more than trite platitudes. Although impressive in quantity, the yield of useful strategies from studies of classroom motivation is, to date, disappointing in number and the extent of classroom-based validation. The ideas which have informed the research are of value in themselves, however, in highlighting the significance of children's perspectives on classrooms, tasks and the ingredients of success for classroom motivation. Nevertheless, useful guidance and strategies are beginning to emerge, but there is an urgent need for research energy to be directed more specifically on the evaluation of classroom-based 'middle range strategies' for supporting and enhancing motivation.

CHAPTER 6

Effective Classroom Behaviour Management

Nigel Hastings and Kevin Wheldall

Doyle (1986) identifies classroom teachers as having just two main tasks: promoting learning and promoting order. Children's behaviour is obviously involved in the second of these, but it is also an element within the first, for, as a recent report concisely stated, 'Good behaviour is a necessary condition for effective teaching and learning, and an important outcome of education' (OFSTED, 1993, p1).

The idea of good behaviour as an educational goal may surprise at first but, whilst schools tend not to treat behaviour as a curriculum subject, most include aspirations for children's conduct among their aims. This is not just a philosophical matter, however. It has a legal basis in England and Wales where the 1988 Education Act gave schools responsibilities for fostering children's social and cultural development and the Education Acts of 1986 and 1993 charge headteachers with 'promoting self-discipline' and 'encouraging good behaviour', as well as with 'otherwise regulating the conduct of pupils'.

Important though good behaviour is as a teaching and learning outcome, our concern in this chapter is with the more instrumental need to establish order in classrooms for effective learning to take place.

Teachers certainly consider that managing children's behaviour is a necessary, important and time-consuming part of their job. Newly qualified teachers throughout the western world report 'classroom discipline' as their main concern (Veenman, 1984, 1987) and many experienced teachers think they spend more time dealing with matters of order and control than they should (Wheldall and Merrett, 1988; Merrett and Wheldall, 1987a; Merrett and Taylor, 1994). Teachers also identify children's misbehaviour as a major source of stress in their work (Pratt, 1978; Boyle et al., 1995). But what is it that children do in classrooms that creates all this concern?

The nature and incidence of troublesome behaviour

The Committee of Enquiry into Discipline in Schools, established in March 1988 and commonly known as the Elton Committee, set out to establish the nature and scale of discipline problems as one of its first tasks. It concluded that none of the available surveys of teachers' beliefs about the state of school discipline had an adequate national sample (see Docking, 1989) and so commissioned its own large-scale survey of teachers' perceptions of the nature and incidence of disruptive behaviour in schools. Drawing for its method on the earlier work of Wheldall, Merrett and their colleagues, the evidence produced the same clear and consistent picture (DES, 1989). Both primary and secondary teachers' day-by-day concerns were the high rates of misbehaviours which, taken individually, are not grave. The most frequent were those Wheldall and Merrett had termed 'TOOT' (talking out of turn, or inappropriate talk) and 'HOC' (hindering other children), along with making unnecessary noise, pushing and shoving, and calculated idleness. More serious acts, such as verbal abuse and physical aggression towards the teacher, were relatively rare. Subsequent studies have found this general pattern repeated elsewhere – in British nursery classes (Merrett and Taylor, 1994), in German primary schools (Schwieso and Ringe, 1990), in Australian primary schools (Johnson, Oswald and Adey, 1993; Wheldall and Beaman, 1994) and even in the classrooms of 50 first and middle school teachers on one of the most remote inhabited islands in the world – St Helena in the South Atlantic! (Jones, Charlton and Wilkin, 1995). These seemingly pan-global behaviours disrupt learning and teaching by their frequency and persistence rather than by their intrinsic natures. Indeed, there is nothing wrong about many of them in other contexts: it is their effects on the learning of the perpetrators and other children, and on teachers' teaching, that makes them inappropriate.

It would be wrong to conclude that primary schools are noisy and ill-disciplined places, however. Research consistently supports the view of HMI (DES, 1987; OFSTED, 1993b) that classrooms are generally well ordered. Observational research in both infant and junior classes repeatedly reveals that children typically spend about 60 per cent of their classroom time engaged with their work, 20 per cent in work-related organisational activities or waiting for their teacher and 20 per cent distracted (for example, Galton, Simon and Croll, 1980).

Some studies have coded children's 'distracted' activities more finely. In the ORACLE research (Galton, Simon and Croll, 1980), disruptive behaviour and horseplay together accounted for well under one per cent of observations of pupil time: similarly low rates were also observed in the Junior School Project (Mortimore et al., 1986). Observations of teachers' involvement in behaviour management can create a different picture, partly because they are managing a whole class of children and partly because they do not only attend to active disruption, they also chivvy passively distracted children. While ORACLE teachers engaged in 'critical control' for just 2.3 per cent of observations, in Leeds schools 10 per cent of teacher–pupil interactions were coded as 'disciplinary', with teachers involved in about 22 disciplinary interactions per hour and the average child in just one (Alexander, 1992). In the more recent Leverhulme Primary Project (Wragg, 1993), the frequency of different types of misbehaviour matched the Elton Committee's questionnaire evidence with 'noisy or illicit talk' and 'inappropriate movement' topping the league table by occurring in 33 per cent and 26 per cent of observed 'segments' (90 second periods); just 2 per cent of misbehaviours were coded as serious and, as in other studies, the great majority of children were well behaved for most of the time.

All of the figures we have considered so far describe the 'average' classroom, but classes vary enormously: rates of disruption and distraction are much lower in some and much higher in others. This variation has emerged in research using teachers' perceptions of frequency and systematic observation methods, as well as in the less structured observational work of inspectors. Differences between classes might be due to class and school intake characteristics, but there is plenty of evidence that what happens in the classroom also has a substantial impact on children's behaviour. Indeed, a recent review concluded that 'the dominant influence on the classroom motivation and behaviour of a very large majority of pupils appears to be the teacher' (Galloway, 1995, p52).

This was also the view of the Elton Committee, which considered that '...teachers' group management skills are probably the single most important factor in achieving good standards of classroom behaviour' (DES, 1989, p70). In writing of 'skills', the Committee endorsed the view that what teachers do can be analysed, learned and improved. It also concluded that the training of teachers in these group management skills was generally inadequate and warranted improvement, a view supported by teachers' assessments of the adequacy of their initial training in classroom behaviour management (Merrett and Wheldall, 1993). A call for more and better training is not difficult to make, but unless there is a research-informed base of knowledge about what teachers can do which promotes good behaviour and reduces the incidence of poor behaviour, further training is likely to be a rather hit-and-miss affair. Fortunately, as the Elton Committee was well aware, a body of relevant evidence does exist.

Classroom behaviour management skills

The Elton Committee identified eleven elements of good practice in classroom behaviour management (DES, 1989, pp71–2). Their list includes points which are well justified by research evidence and others derived from collective professional judgement and experience. We will concentrate on the extensive research evidence on classroom processes and their relationships to pupil behaviour.

It is easier to organise, digest and use this evidence if it is set within a framework. We find the A-B-C model, which has been widely used in research and writing on behaviour management, helpful for this purpose (Wheldall and Merrett, 1984; Merrett and Wheldall, 1990). The model embodies a simple distinction between two types of classroom influence on behaviour – *Antecedents*, which happen or are in place before the target *Behaviour*, and events which follow it, the *Consequences*.

The merits of this A-B-C framework are:

(i) It focuses attention on what children actually *do*. The 'B' is the behaviour in question – such as chatting or wandering around – rather than a general evaluative label such as 'disruptive'.

(ii) It also directs attention to events *within the classroom* where teachers' influence is greatest. What happens in children's lives outside the classroom certainly influences their behaviour in school but, at least in the short term, these are matters over which a class teacher can do little.

(iii) It emphasises that children's behaviour, both appropriate and inappropriate, takes place in a context. Children respond to what is going on and, through their behaviour, influence what happens next.

(iv) It helps in drawing an important distinction between the *identification* and the *explanation* of links between classroom process and children's behaviour. Although the A-B-C model has historical connections with behaviourism and applied behaviour analysis, its use does not require a commitment to or acceptance of any particular explanatory framework.

(v) Finally, and most importantly, it is a simple and useful tool for thinking about the complex business of managing classroom behaviour.

We have already discussed the types of behaviour which primary teachers' would generally like to reduce in frequency. The 'tools' available for use in establishing order and minimising or reducing the frequency of these behaviours – the '*B*s' in the model – are the '*A*s' and the '*C*s'. We will take each in turn and summarise some of the main evidence of links with the incidence of troublesome behaviour.

Antecedents of classroom behaviour: the '*A*s'

In his comprehensive and widely cited review of classroom organisation and management, Doyle (1986) concludes that:

> ...classroom management is fundamentally a process of solving the problem of order in classrooms rather than the problems of misbehaviour or student engagement....Indeed, high engagement and low levels of inappropriate and disruptive behaviour are by-products of an effective program of classroom organisation and management. (p423)

In doing so, he highlights the significance of establishing order as an active rather than reactive process in teaching. Teachers set and shape the conditions for children to work in and also for them to misbehave in. Research has identified a number of relationships, not all of them straightforward, between these conditions and rates of misbehaviour or time spent on- and off-task.

Curriculum tasks

Doyle's two goals of teaching – promoting learning and promoting order – are inevitably closely related in practice. Actions taken to promote learning will often influence behaviour as well. Nowhere is this more immediately obvious than in the likely effects of the work children are required to do. The general expectation is that if work is undemanding, repetitious, dull and boring, children will find something more interesting to do: wandering around, chatting or daydreaming might each provide relief from the tedium. Similarly, it is often suggested that a functional reaction to fear of failure or to an incomprehensible or very hard task is to engage in some 'off-task' activity instead.

We would not wish to underplay the importance of the curriculum, but Bennett et al. (1984) found infants and young juniors were remarkably tolerant of a 'staple diet of little new knowledge and large amounts of practice' (p213). They also found that although teachers tended to notice when tasks were too demanding for children and make adjustments, they were 'totally blind to tasks whose demands were too easy' (p215) as their children were generally industrious and worked cheerfully. The same general picture also emerges from the more recent PACE evidence (Pollard et al., 1994). The reason so many children do not start to misbehave in these circumstances may lie in their understanding of the purposes of classroom life. As many have pointed out, children's ideas about the purpose of classroom tasks may not be learning but pleasing their teacher by working diligently in exchange for undemanding tasks.

So, although it can be no justification for a dull curriculum, the widespread idea that uninteresting, undemanding work leads to boredom which is relieved through 'TOOTing', 'HOCing' and otherwise being off-task, is not well supported by this evidence from the early primary years, even though the links may hold for some individuals.

Tasks and contexts

One aspect of primary classroom practice which evidence indicates has a substantial impact on the time that children spend working, daydreaming or more actively disrupting events, is the match between the nature of a learning task and the context in which it is to be done. The most common mis-match is between individual tasks and the social context provided by group seating arrangements, and its consequences are marked. In fact, for the children whose behaviour generally causes most concern, they are little short of devastating. We will not dwell further on this important matter here as the evidence is fully reviewed in Chapter 3.

Task management

In addition to the content of tasks and the contexts in which they are undertaken, aspects of the ways in which teachers manage the curriculum and focus children's attention on work have also been found to relate to classroom behaviour. The effects of task and classroom management on learning have been well researched and comprehensive reviews are provided by Walberg (1986), Brophy and Good (1986) and Creemers (1994). Generally, teaching strategies that are effective in promoting learning are also effective in minimising disruption and distraction, but few studies have examined effects on behaviour directly. One highly influential exception is Kounin's (1970) analysis of video recordings of classes of five to eight year olds which identified differences in the class management strategies of teachers with high and low rates of disruption and off-task behaviours in their classes.

Teachers with less disruption gave their pupils the (correct) impression that they knew what was going on in every corner of the classroom, a skill described by Kounin as *withitness*. First, they scanned the teaching area more frequently than most and, in doing so, gained information about classroom activities and made momentary eye-contact, perhaps particularly with those who were not engrossed in their work. Second, these teachers thought aloud, reviewing their plans for the session and its progress for all to hear. From this slightly eccentric monologue children would correctly gain the impression that their teacher was in control of events and be repeatedly reminded of the structure and development of the session.

Every lesson or teaching session has episodes within it. A common pattern in primary classrooms is for a teacher-led introductory phase, followed by group or individual work and a concluding procedural episode of clearing up. Kounin found that his more successful teachers attended to the *flow and momentum* of the session, alerted children to its sequence and structure, and made clear, well signalled and *smooth transitions* from one episode to the next.

The study also revealed that teachers with more task-involved classes made greater use of *overlapping*, the skill of doing more than one thing at a time, particularly when dealing with minor disruptive behaviour. For example, while listening to and continuing to look at a child reporting on his group's recent discussion, a teacher deals with another absentmindedly 'zizzing' the velcro strip on her shoe by moving to stand by her and discretely wagging a finger. Teachers with more off-task behaviour in their classes were more likely to stop the session to deal with misbehaviour and then have to re-focus attention to get started again. The net effect of the more successful teachers' skills was to focus attention on work.

Although Kounin's evidence is strictly only correlational, his findings are consistent with those emerging from many subsequent studies. Mortimore et al. (1986) reported better behaviour and more task involvement in classes in which teachers sustained a 'work-centred environment' and Wragg (1993) describes a similar pattern. In their study of American junior high school English teachers, Doyle and Carter (1987) also identified a strong work focus among their better classroom managers who not only acted differently in the classroom but also, so it emerged from interviews, thought differently about classroom teaching. 'Successful classroom managers, it would appear, tend to think about classrooms in terms of activities and movement, whereas less successful managers tend to concentrate on individual student contacts' (p90).

Teacher–pupil interaction

The extent to which teachers concentrate their time on interactions with individuals compared with groups and the class as a whole has been shown to relate to classroom behaviour and a number of other educational outcomes (see Chapter 2). Galton, Simon and Croll (1980) found a strong association between teacher interaction patterns and children's behaviour, together with a clear indication that it is teachers' behaviour which influences the children's, rather than vice-versa. In general, classes taught by teachers who spent more time in class interaction were more work-engaged and less distracted, while classes taught by teachers who spent more time in one-to-one interactions spent less time working and more time off-task. Consistent with this, Mortimore et al. (1986) found associations between children's involvement with their work and both the proportion of time teachers spent in whole class interaction and with the time teachers spent in any kind of interaction with children.

This pattern has been repeated in the findings of two subsequent studies in English primary classrooms. Croll and Moses' (1988) observations of 32 junior classrooms yielded strong correlations between the proportion of whole class interaction and children's time on-task (0.65) as well as distraction (–0.58). However, it was not just that children spent more time on-task in the whole class sessions, they were also less distracted when they were working alone on their individual tasks. The PACE Key Stage 1 research has also found less distraction and more work involvement in classes with high levels of class interaction.

The important point to note from this evidence is that the issue is not about whether it is more effective for classroom management to engage in whole class, group or individual interactions, it is the *balance* between the three which seems to be an important influence on children's behaviour and attention as well as their learning. This evidence sits comfortably with the work on task management discussed earlier and with Doyle and Carter's observation that more effective classroom managers view and operate with their classes as entities and not just as a gathering of individuals.

Classroom rules and routines

The final antecedent to be considered is classroom rules. All classes have rules and, especially at the start of each year with a new class, teachers focus on the rules and routines. For a class to operate in an orderly way, all involved have to learn and generally comply with the conventions and systems. Wragg (1993) describes the first three days of 20 teachers with their new classes. A strong emphasis on rules and procedures, on induction into and instruction in the ways of the new class was evident. Analysis of fifty of the rules being established in these first class meetings showed that three-quarters concerned resources, classroom procedures and noise. Nearly half were introduced by 'direct command' and all were teacher led.

Although children may infringe rules, they have no problem with their place in school. Cullingford's (1988) interviewees left him in no doubt that they thought rules are essential and that vital elements of a teacher's job are inventing and maintaining rules and dispensing punishments to wrong doers. Their ideas about why rules are necessary reflected a somewhat grim view of human nature, however. Rather than thinking of them as helpful to the development of self-control and as becoming less necessary as children grow older, these philosophers thought that more and stronger rules would be needed to contain an increasing tendency to 'wickedness' in their secondary schools.

Classroom rules have tended to be implicit but there has been a resurgence of interest in making some explicit, though the rationale for doing so stands in marked contrast with Cullingford's children's ideas. The argument for explicit rules is that there is nothing particularly 'natural' about good classroom behaviour: children have to learn the rules and procedures, particularly about when, where and at what volume they can talk to whom about what. The Elton Report (DES, 1989), OFSTED (1993b) and DfE (1994) all commend the development of clear expectations for pupils' behaviour, expressed in the form of rules and at both whole school and class levels, and there is evidence that most primary schools now have, or are currently developing, explicit school rule structures (Merrett and Jones, 1994). At present there is no evidence of the extent to which explicit rules are used in classrooms but, as with school rules, there seems to be growing professional endorsement of their value. The consensus among writers of primary teaching texts is that the list should be limited to a maximum of five or six rules, worded as aspirations rather than prohibitions, and be developed by the children. Praise for keeping to the rules is also strongly advocated.

No research has examined whether behaviour is better when children have developed the rules themselves, or when rules are expressed positively rather than negatively, desirable though these approaches might be on educational grounds. However, many studies demonstrate improved behaviour following use of rules *and* praise for rule compliance ('Yes Rehana, you've got your hand up, what did you think?'; 'It's good to see everyone keeping our first rule about trying to work quietly.' See Merrett, 1981, 1993). Additionally, evaluations of training programmes in classroom behaviour management which involve a rules and praise approach also indicate its value in supporting more orderly classroom behaviour and increased time on-task (Wheldall, Merrett and Borg, 1985; Nicholls and Houghton, 1995). Used without praise, however, rules have no appreciable effect on behaviour (Madsen, Becker and Thomas, 1968).

Most research on the effects of classroom rules has taken the form of intervention studies in which teachers have changed their practice by introducing explicit rules and praise. The overwhelming majority of published reports indicate that worthwhile changes in time on-task and in the frequency of disruptive behaviour follow. We can therefore claim with some confidence that rules can play an important role in establishing and maintaining order in the classroom, but not on their own. They must be used with recognition for rule keeping if they are to influence classroom behaviour. Unfortunately, our experience and anecdotal evidence is that many primary teachers have introduced classroom rules and displayed them prominently expecting that this alone would change classroom behaviour, only to be disappointed by the lack of impact. Rules provide only the framework of clear expectations and aspirations. To impact on behaviour, they must be consistently applied, with due regard for the context, and be supported by recognition and praise for rule keeping.

To summarise so far, the evidence strongly supports the proposition that effective behaviour management is not just a matter of how misbehaviour is dealt with. The ways in which teachers plan, organise and implement the curriculum and the classroom, their patterns of interaction with children and the attention they give to establishing and maintaining the rules and routines all influence the amount of disruptive behaviour that will take place.

Consequences for classroom behaviour: the '*C*s'

Whilst the 'Antecedents' we have considered are important components in classroom behaviour management, the ways in which teachers notice and respond to children's behaviour are also important. The most obvious way is reprimanding misbehaviour but, as we noted when considering classroom rules, providing consequences for good behaviour is an important part of a teacher's repertoire. We will take each type in turn.

Responding to misbehaviour

However good a teacher's classroom management skills, some misbehaviour will always arise. Like accidents on the road, the frequency and severity of disruption in the classroom can be reduced but it will never be eliminated. The question then is what should a teacher do when misbehaviour happens? There are moral and educational dimensions to this question, but our concern can be only with the effects of teachers' responses which mostly take the form of a comment, but sometimes involve arranging a punishment, such as staying in at playtime, being referred to the head or a letter being sent home. Two sorts of effect have to be considered, the short term and the long term. Ideally, a reprimand will both stop the behaviour at the time and also prevent its recurrence.

Kounin (1970) found that teachers' normal 'desist' strategies generally work: children stopped when told to, at least in the short term. Wragg's (1993) analysis of events in 60 primary classes shows that teachers responded to misbehaviour, usually inappropriate talk or movement, by an order for it to cease, naming the pupil(s) and/or issuing a reprimand. The episodes were generally dealt with briefly, calmly and almost always before escalation and, in all but 5 per cent of cases, misbehaviour ceased or lessened immediately. The short term is not a problem. The difficulty is, as the Elton Committee (DES, 1989) noted, that misbehaviours such as TOOT, HOC and wandering around recur and, in doing so, show that the long-term effects of normal desist responses are, at best, limited. If this were not the case, we might expect that the teachers who criticised more frequently would come to have lower rates of misbehaviour, but precisely the reverse tends to be the case. Indeed, the indications are that the more critical a teacher becomes, the less children will interpret the litany of complaints as having to do with their behaviour and the more they will incline to interpreting them as evidence of their teacher's miserable, moaning disposition (Worrall, Worrall and Meldrum, 1983), in the same way that nagging is often taken as a pathology of the nagger rather than a reflection of the nagged's behaviour. Frequent negative comments have their predictable consequences for classroom relationships and atmosphere.

Rather than respond to misbehaviour, another possibility is to ignore it. Indeed, some advocate ignoring misbehaviour on the grounds that attention, albeit critical attention, may reinforce it. A well tried strategy within the broad field of behaviour management is known as Rules, Praise and Ignore (RPI) in which clear expectations are established, praise is given for rule compliance and (safe) rule breaking is ignored: Merrett and Wheldall (1990) and Merrett (1993) give examples of its successful use. However, there are reasons for caution in embarking on an approach involving ignoring misbehaviour. First, there need to be grounds for believing that troublesome behaviour is being maintained by the attention which normal reprimands are providing. Second, as well as questions of effectiveness, there are issues of justice to consider and some misbehaviours may warrant censure by virtue of their nature alone, irrespective of whether that censure 'works'.

There can be occasions when it is appropriate to ignore misbehaviour and 'turn a blind eye' for other reasons, however. Doyle and Carter

(1987) noted that some of their most successful classroom managers ignored misbehaviour, particularly at the start of the session when they were focusing attention on the curriculum tasks, and, in many cases, the momentum they were developing for the lesson swamped the misbehaviour as children became involved.

To summarise, children generally stop 'normal misbehaviour' when told to, particularly when it is picked up early. As a way of bringing about longer-term improvements in classroom behaviour, however, teachers' normal practices of instructions to desist and reprimands are of limited value alone. Evidence also supports the intuitive supposition that the more frequent critical comment on behaviour becomes, the less effect it has on misbehaviour and the more adverse become the consequences for classroom relationships.

Responding to good behaviour

Teachers generally believe that it is important to praise children for progress and achievement in learning, but the idea of extending this strategy to children's behaviour has become widely canvassed in recent years. Praise is not the only way in which approval for appropriate behaviour might be given; badges, 'smiley' stickers and commendations are also used, but they are usually accompanied by praise and it is therefore on praise that we will focus.

Studies of primary teachers' use of praise and criticism yield a varied picture of normal practice. The ORACLE and Junior School projects (Galton et al., 1980; Mortimore et al., 1986), using the same observation system, both recorded work related praise in 1 per cent of observations and Tizard et al. (1988) observed a similarly low level in infant classes. All three found statements of critical control to be more frequent. In contrast, Merrett and Wheldall (1987b), using a schedule designed specifically to focus on 'positive' and 'negative' teacher interactions, found positives to be slightly more frequent in 128 English primary and middle school classes, though in a later study (Merrett and Wheldall, 1992) they found the reverse. Inconsistencies in findings reflect differences in observation systems, considerable differences between teachers and possibly the time when observations were made, as teachers tend to become less positive and more negative in their comments as a school term progresses, especially with children identified as having behaviour difficulties (Fry, 1983, 1987).

In general, British primary children think they get about the right amount of both praise and criticism (Merrett and Tang, 1994) and, contrary to popular belief and some earlier evidence, boys do not seem to get more positive or negative attention than girls (Merrett and Wheldall, 1992). Croll's (1985) analysis of interaction in junior classes showed that where boys received more teacher attention than girls, it was related to the fact that more boys had learning or behaviour difficulties and, as Moses discusses in Chapter 8, children with learning and behaviour difficulties tend to get more teacher attention.

The most significant finding from studies of teachers' normal rates of praise and disapproval concerns the way these are distributed between work and conduct. Merrett and Wheldall's studies in particular have revealed a remarkably consistent pattern. Praise is used predominantly for work and criticism for behaviour. Criticism for work is used sparingly; but, other than with the youngest classes, teachers rarely praise for good behaviour. Alongside this, Wheldall, Merrett and their associates have also repeatedly demonstrated in classroom intervention studies how the behaviour and on-task levels of individual pupils and whole classes can improve when teachers increase their praise for appropriate behaviour and for working. (See Merrett and Wheldall (1990); Merrett (1993); Wheldall and Glynn (1989) for illustrative case studies.)

However, praise is not a magic potion. It is a powerful tool in a teacher's repertoire but only if used with discretion, sensitivity and skill for, as Brophy (1981) cautions, praise can also discourage. There are important developmental changes in children's understanding of teachers' praise and criticism. Five year olds will glow when praised, believing their teacher thinks they are clever, hard-working and good. Ten year olds are more discerning. For them, praise for a modest achievement may signal a teacher's judgement of low ability, just as criticism can serve as a high ability cue (Barker and Graham, 1987; Butler, 1994; and see Chapter 5).

Bearing in mind the developmental changes in children's interpretations of praise, the research is sufficient to inform the development of general guidance for its effective use. Brophy (1981) offers a list of 12 suggestions; ours is limited to four.

1. Praise should be *contingent, frequent and immediate*. Being indiscriminately 'nice' by oozing positive comments is useless. Praise must relate to particular behaviours and be delivered when they happen. In the early stages of establishing a pattern of behaviour, a new routine for example, praise should be frequent. Once behaviour is at an appropriate level, the frequency can be reduced. Rules that are generally kept require only occasional support through praise.
2. Praise must carry *information about the accomplishment*. It should not just provide a glow, it needs to carry information about what it is

that is being applauded. Particularly with children older than about eight years, the focus should be on praise for improvement rather than for performance, especially where the achievement is unexceptional by class standards: 'Well done blue group, you've cleared up much more quickly this time'.

3. From the ideas and evidence discussed more fully in Chapter 5, we can infer that praise for improved behaviour should sometimes include *internal attributions*, whereby responsibility for good or improved behaviour is attributed to children's efforts or increasing ability.
4. Finally, praise should be given with *sensitivity* to the individuals concerned. Public announcements lead some children to swell with pride and others to wither in embarrassment or anxiety.

Conclusion

Order is essential for learning: creating and maintaining order are essential in teaching. The evidence we have reviewed highlights clear relationships between things teachers do, or can do, and children's behaviour in class, particularly the proportion of time they spend engaged with their work. The detail of these studies is important, but the general picture is that classrooms in which teachers generate and sustain a strong work-focus; establish clear sets of expectations, routines and rules which are consistently applied; distribute their interactions so that every child is engaged with them for more than a small proportion of his or her time; and arrange for seating to match tasks, are classrooms where high levels of task engagement and lower levels of distraction, TOOTing, HOCing and other routine troublesome misbehaviours are likely to be found.

Inevitably, however, no matter how ideal the antecedents, there will always be some distracted and troublesome behaviour in any primary classroom. Teachers who also acknowledge good behaviour and use praise in the ways indicated are likely to maintain both high levels of appropriate behaviour and task engagement in their classes. They are also likely to enjoy their teaching and have a better relationship with their class than if they respond only to inappropriate behaviour. However, it may be reassuring to know that the evidence does not support any call for teachers only to say positive things to children! Although the long-term effects of normal classroom reprimands and desist instructions are not encouraging, studies in which teachers tried periods of being *only* positive found both work and classroom behaviour were *worse* than when both appropriate and inappropriate behaviour were commented on (Rosen et al., 1984;

Pfiffner, Rosen and O'Leary, 1985; Pfiffner and O'Leary, 1987).

Misbehaviour in the classroom wears teachers down, of this there is no doubt. It also interferes with learning. But the encouraging picture to emerge clearly from research is, once again, that what teachers do matters: they substantially affect the amounts of disruption, distraction and good behaviour that take place. Moreover, this picture highlights the types of classroom strategy which are of proven worth in establishing and maintaining order in classrooms and warrant development and refinement within every primary teacher's professional repertoire.

CHAPTER 7

Teaching Reading in the Primary Classroom

Rhona Stainthorp

Introduction

An analysis of the titles of the chapters in this book might raise a question about the inclusion of the teaching of reading. After all, this is not a book about the curriculum and reading is now specifically Attainment Target 2 of the English Curriculum. However, it is possible to argue that reading is not a curriculum *subject* at all, but a skill that has to be acquired in order to access the rest of the curriculum. This means that teaching children to read is one of the most important aspects of the primary teacher's job. Thus, not surprisingly, when Her Majesty's Inspectorate (HMI) reported on the teaching of reading in 1991 they found that '...the primary schools give a high priority to teaching children to read in Key Stage 1 (5 to 7 year olds)' (DES, 1991, p2). This would no doubt be the case in the majority of primary schools around the world. Learning to read is seen as an essential part of and prerequisite for much school learning.

This chapter will review evidence from experimental cognitive developmental psychology about what children need to learn in order to become skilled readers. It will then consider evidence from training studies about the effects of using the empirical evidence to inform teaching. The focus will be on the early years; on learning to read the words. This is done acknowledging that we generally read words in contexts. However, in order to read an unknown word in context, that context itself has to be read and therefore may be of little use to the beginning reader with poor word reading skills. For a skilled reader, the act of reading is automatic and the means by which the print is processed are no longer available for reflection. Empirical evidence from psychological experiments sheds light on this and can be used to inform teachers about effective teaching strategies. The chapter can only present a tiny slice of the multifaceted nature of reading but reference is made to sources giving a fuller treatment of particular aspects of the field.

HMI and 'Good practice'

By way of scene setting, it is fair to say that the teaching of reading received a good deal of media coverage in the late 1980s which continued into the early 1990s. Putting it crudely, there was an argument about whether the teaching of reading was dominated by adherence to a particular method. The suggestion was that teachers had moved towards using a 'psycholinguistic' approach whereby children were encouraged to use contextual cues to guess at the text of a wide variety of individual books, written without pedagogy in mind – so-called 'real books'. This was considered to have been at the expense of a skills-based approach dominated by 'phonics'. There were advocates of both extremes; McNee (1990) pressing for phonics first and Waterland (1985) wanting an apprenticeship approach based on 'real books'. However, this advocacy tended to be based on passion rather than empirical evidence.

Further fuel for the 'reading debate' was added by the publication of *Sponsored Reading Failure* by Turner (1990). He suggested that there was evidence from performance on reading tests from nine unnamed LEAs that (a) reading standards were falling; (b) the teaching of reading was moving towards a 'real books' approach; and (c) the two were causally related in that where a 'real books' approach was used it was associated with falling standards. Any publication that suggests that there are falling standards is bound to get considerable media coverage.

One of the problems with this 'debate' was that it was possible for opinion to flourish in the absence of data because we did not, indeed we still do not, have any national data on reading performance. A recent briefing paper from the National Commission on Education (Brooks, Foxman and Gorman, 1995) points out that until an effective system of monitoring of educational standards throughout the country is in place, arguments about standards will continue to flourish. What we do have is official reports from HMI. These result from inspections of schools where the inspectors assess the quality of learning and relate it to the quality of the teaching they observe. They specifically make comments about effective schools and 'good practice'. An analysis of the reports relating to reading published in 1978, 1990, 1991 and 1993 serves to highlight the problem for teachers in trying to establish effective teaching strategies for developing reading competence.

The 1978 report *Primary Education in England* (DES, 1978b) did not focus on reading *per se*, but the teaching of reading was included. HMI felt it was dependent on structured reading schemes and the subtext of the report is that this was a weakness and not 'good practice'. HMI acknowledged that the approach had resulted in children having good basic reading skills, but they were not considered to be having a rich enough diet of reading experiences across a wide range of genres and quality authors. The message from the 1978 survey was that teachers needed to extend the range whilst still ensuring that the basic skills were acquired. As we shall discuss below, the amount of reading that a child does is crucial to the development of skilled performance.

Twelve years later, in *The teaching and learning of language and literacy* (DES, 1990), HMI reported that reading schemes were still widely used, but with greater discrimination. They found that the basic skills of reading and writing continued to receive a great deal of attention in primary schools. However, they commented that in schools where these were given '...an undue prominence' (p7) the standards were considered to be good, but only on a narrow front.

This report presents us with little vignettes of 'good practice', but these imply rather than state how HMI consider reading might be taught. Examples include the setting up of environments, talking about books, even reading books, but there is no description in depth of how reading should really be taught.

In 1990, the effective school was considered by HMI to be one where early reading was '...structured and enjoyable' (DES, 1990, p30) and children were encouraged to reflect upon their reading. Right from the beginning of their schooling, the children would '...read for meaning and read a large variety of materials including picture books, stories, poems and books of information' (p30). Such a school was one where no particular reading scheme was used exclusively and even when schemes were used they were supplemented by '...good quality fiction and non-fiction' (p30). The implication, as far as HMI are concerned, is that reading scheme books cannot be good books. In contrast, Perera (1993), in analysing what makes a good book, found that the characteristics of a good read were just as likely to be found amongst reading scheme books as amongst 'real books'.

This 1990 HMI report does not give a detailed description of what is involved in teaching reading. It gives the impression that by being provided with a book rich environment where reading is integrated with other language activities and by listening to and reading a wide range of literature, children will somehow succeed. In all fairness to HMI this was a report about *Language and Literacy*, not specifically the teaching of reading and they clearly set out to give a broad brush account of what they had found in schools over the decade.

Then Turner's pamphlet was published. This prompted the Secretary of State to commission another report and in 1991 *The teaching and learning of reading in primary schools: a report by HMI* (Autumn 1990) was published. This had been asked for because of '...widespread expressions of concern about reading standards and teaching methods in primary schools' (DES, 1991, p1). The Turner pamphlet with its resulting media hype must be seen as causal in this because there was no hint of any widespread concern about teaching methods and standards of reading in the 1990 survey.

In order to prepare the new report, HMI brought forward to the Autumn term of 1990 the inspection of 120 schools which had been scheduled for the following year. The brief was that HMI should specifically focus on teaching approaches and the reading standards associated with them. They observed reading being taught in 470 classes and heard over 2,000 children read aloud. The document reports that standards were satisfactory or better in 80 per cent of schools and high in 30 per cent of those. This left 20 per cent with poor standards. HMI acknowledged that this was not cause for complacency, but felt that it was not evidence of falling standards. Presumably this view was based on what might be called 'clinical' judgement as the exact criteria by which standards were assessed are not discussed (see Pumfrey, 1995, for a discussion of this).

In order to investigate pedagogy, HMI studied the schools' written policy documents and questioned the teachers about their approaches. They found no evidence of either schools or individual teachers changing to using single approaches. Nearly 85 per cent were using a blend of methods and less than 18 per cent used any single method predominantly. The single methods that they cite were 'phonics', 'look-and-say' and 'real books'. They found that 95 per cent were using a reading scheme and almost all taught phonics. This report was therefore considerably more specific about how teaching was being carried out than the previous year's report. For example, the 1990 report had made no mention of phonics.

HMI observed a clear link between higher standards and systematic phonics teaching *provided* that it was being taught in such a way that the children were able to apply their knowledge to the acts of reading and writing. There is a hint that some schools were judged to be introducing phonics too late. They comment that teachers often introduced phonics when a child was considered to be failing, when it might have been more fruitful if it had been incorporated from the start.

Only 5 per cent of teachers described their approach as 'real books' and are gently damned by this report. HMI appreciated that their children had a great interest in books, but felt that they had made too little progress. They were judged able to tell the story of the book, but reading accuracy was '...too limited because they had too few skills in decoding print.' This meant that '...they were ill-equipped to move on to unfamiliar material, for example non-fiction texts. Moreover, they were weak readers of instructions and questions in subjects such as mathematics' (DES, 1991, p7). HMI, therefore, had found no evidence that the schools were espousing a 'real books' approach in any wholesale way, but those that had were not considered to be examples of 'good practice'.

This report was much more explicit about what 'good practice' was considered to be. In Year R it was where the children listened to stories, were introduced to the reading scheme materials, learnt an initial vocabulary through labels and captions, learnt letter names and sounds, engaged in language play based on speech patterns, rhyme and jingles and worked on phonics programmes that highlight initial sounds. There had been a considerable shift in emphasis between 1990 and 1991. The same sort of shift is evident in their characterisation of 'good practice' in Years 1 and 2. For these Years it was where the children read their graded scheme books and then consolidated their skills by reading a wide range of authors and genres at the same level. The teachers ensured that sight vocabulary was reinforced through using word banks and dictionaries and that decoding skills were continuing to be developed through the teaching of letter combinations for sounds. Economy of effort was achieved through ensuring that these skills were used for access to new words and for developing writing. In order to ensure that reading was perceived as a generative activity, good teachers increasingly used written instructions to consolidate and even replace verbal instructions across the curriculum. Their observations dovetailed with the requirements of AT2.

In 1993 there was yet another report, *The teaching and learning of reading and writing in Reception Classes and Year 1* (OFSTED, 1993c). This was designed to complement the previous two surveys, but was on a much smaller scale. A new aspect of the learning of reading was highlighted this time. The concentration on the early years brought into sharp focus the fact that the socio-economic background of the children and their pre-school experiences in literacy had a marked effect on early performance. There was, however, an interaction between home and school. Schools with the best teaching, when they happened to be in advantaged areas, were able to achieve the highest standards, whereas the children who came from the most disadvantaged homes were doubly jeopardised if they had poor teaching.

And the most skilful teaching? This tended to be in Year R where the teachers had ensured that the children had been introduced to the first books of the reading scheme and had learnt a basic vocabulary which enabled them to start reading the books with a high level of success. They were also teaching the children '...initial phonic sounds' (p2). HMI observed that in the good schools 'All the teachers used structured reading schemes as the backbone of their approach' (p6). It was also noted that in two thirds of the classes, the teaching of phonics was '...systematic, regular and progressive' (p6). In the one third of classes where this was judged to be the most effective, the teachers were ensuring that the children were able to apply their knowledge when reading and writing.

It would seem from these last two reports that HMI have identified using a considered 'balanced approach', combining the use of a reading scheme or schemes with a graded vocabulary and direct teaching of phonics to ensure accuracy and independence as being 'good practice'; consolidation of skill at all stages being ensured through reading a wide variety of genres integrated with discussion and focused writing. From a reading of these last two reports, practising teachers will have a clear view of what the HMI now consider to be effective teaching. However, they could be forgiven for feeling that 'good practice' is based on fashion rather than evidence. The very considerable shift in the emphasis HMI give to different aspects of 'good practice' between 1990 and 1993 is not explained and no account of the nature of reading acquisition is given to justify it.

Research evidence on reading

Teachers and students in training might find that they need to have more than generalised observational data to feel satisfied that they are teaching in the most effective manner. Operating professionally means they need to do more than implement a prescribed approach. A knowledge of any theoretical underpinning of a teaching approach can make for rational teaching. They have the National Curriculum as a guide to what has to be taught, but professionalism requires that teachers do not just follow a recipe slavishly. They have to be flexible in order to take account of individual needs.

A model of the word reading process that has informed much research on reading has been characterised as the **Dual Route Model**. This is a model of *skilled* word reading, but it can help us to understand the processes that children need to establish in order to *become* skilled readers in an alphabetic system. The model suggests that when skilled readers see words they can both *recognise* them, because they have stored representations of them, and *work them out* by parsing the printed word into units called GRAPHEMES, which map onto the units of sound called PHONEMES. Teachers may liken this to using letter-sound correspondences. The resulting phoneme strings are then blended together to result in words. For example, the written word SHEEP can be parsed into three graphemic units, SH, EE and P which map onto the three phonemes / sh /, / ee / and / p /.

The 'recognising' route is called the **Direct Lexical Access Route**. If words can be read by this route, they can be considered to be part of the visual recognition vocabulary, sometimes called the *visual lexicon*. The lexicon is the language system where words are 'stored'. Each word in a person's lexicon can be conceived of as having three identities: *semantic* – its meaning, *syntactic* – its grammatical class; and *phonological* – what it sounds like. Once a word has been learnt visually, a fourth identity can be considered to have been added. This is the *orthographic identity* – what it looks like, its graphemic structure. All these identities must be interconnected so that, on hearing a known word, a literate person should be able to say what it means, how it is spelt, and be able to place it in a sentence frame that implies its syntactic class. The same happens when reading a known word, the other three identities should become available. It is only possible to read a word by this route if that word is already known, as recognition is dependent on there being a stored orthographic identity.

The 'working out' route is called the **Sublexical Route**. A word's constituent letter string is parsed into graphemes which are mapped directly onto phonemes to give a string of phonemes that can be blended to form the word's phonology. For example the word CHIP can be parsed into CH I and P which map onto the sounds / ch / / i / and / p /. Reading a word by this route is not dependent on there being a stored representation. We know that skilled readers can use this route because they can read non-words. A non-word is a string of letters that do not map onto any word in the language; e.g. CLONT or CRINT.

There is evidence that skilled readers have the two routes available. Ability to read non-words shows they can use the sublexical route and ability to pronounce irregular words correctly shows they can use the direct lexical access route. An irregular word is one whose spelling does not map directly onto its pronunciation; e.g. YACHT and COLONEL. The output from the sublexical route will lead to a mispronunciation of these words. Children often make what are called regularisation errors when they are moving into a stage of becoming skilled readers. This means that they appear to use the output from the sublexical route so that an irregular word like COUNTRY may be pronounced with the first vowel as in COUNT. This would suggest that they do not yet have a stored representation of the word.

Frith (1985) has suggested that when children first begin to learn to read they may treat written words very much like other visual stimuli in the environment. It may be that they are told the word that is represented by the sequence of letters and they will then seek some idiosyncratic feature to act as a cue for subsequent recall. They tend not to pay attention to the whole visual sequence. Frith calls this reading **Logographic.** The child treats the visual sequence as a single unit and tries to recognise it using partial cues. This strategy can be very successful. Gough, Juel and Griffith (1992) asked 32 four and five year olds to learn a series of single words on individual cards. (This is analogous to what still happens in many schools where teachers give children a series of words on cards to build up their recognition vocabulary.) The particular aspect of this experiment that is of interest here was that on one of the cards there was a thumbprint. After the children had achieved the criterion of two 100 per cent correct runs without help, they were shown a card with the 'thumbprint' word on, but this time, there was no distinguishing mark. Less than half the children were able to identify the word. However, when they were shown a further card with a thumbprint on in the same place but a different word, nearly all of them identified it as being the original 'thumbprint' word. This is good evidence that some children use a partial visual strategy to try to remember the words. If children are taught by a wholly look-and-say approach, they may appear to achieve success, but eventually there will be too many words which are too alike to be distinguishable. They need some other strategy for differentiating between and recognising *all* words.

Being able to work out the phonology of any new word by mapping letters onto sounds, thus developing the sublexical route, is such a strategy. This level of insight is important because, without an ability to decode unknown words, the child will be always dependent on other people for support. Once the sublexical route is established, new regular words will be correctly identified. Also, the best first estimate of an irregular word can be refined with context and support from a listener. The fact that English contains words whose orthography is opaque in this way has been used to decry the use of phonics in teaching. However, even a unique word like YACHT is not devoid of phonic clues in its spelling. The initial Y is always pronounced / j / and the final T is always pronounced / t /. If learners can work out the consonant frame it is possible to refine the vowel sound using lexical knowledge and context. It is only when they have no knowledge of how to use letter-sound correspondences to work out words that they have problems.

A longitudinal study by Stuart and Coltheart (1988) demonstrates this perfectly. They made a detailed analysis of the errors that a group of children made when reading single words that they had already encountered in their reading instruction. The data were collected on seven occasions beginning two months after the children had started Infant school and ending eighteen months later. This provided a database of some 4,000 errors which could be analysed for evidence of the strategies the children were using.

There were five types of errors. The first type bore little similarity to the target word; e.g. see HER and say '*boy*'. These errors tended to be made by children with low reading ages and little knowledge about letter names and sounds. The second type might have shared one or more letters with the target word, but they would be out of position; e.g. HOME read as '*shop*'. The third type was where the final letter(s) were shared with the target; e.g. LOVE read as '*have*'. Both these types of error tended to be made by children with low reading ages but who had slightly more letter-sound knowledge than the children making type 1 errors. These three error types were considered to be 'bad' in that they did not reflect an understanding of how the spelling system works. They were also associated with children who had made little progress in reading.

The remaining two types of errors could be classified as 'good'. The fourth type of error was where the mistake and the target word shared the initial letter(s) with the target word; e.g. ONE read as '*on*'. The final type was where the error shared at least the initial and final letters with the target; e.g. GRASS read as '*guess*'. These types of error were made by children who had good letter-sound knowledge and who had made greater progress in reading.

Because this was a longitudinal study, Stuart and Coltheart were able to track the patterns of errors that individual children made and map these onto their reading performance, letter-sound knowledge and phonological awareness. Those children who had good letter knowledge and who were phonologically aware from the start were the ones who made good progress in reading and their errors tended to fall into types 4 and 5 – the 'good' errors. They appeared to have started reading using an alphabetic strategy. Those children who had difficulty in learning letter-sound correspondences and in becoming aware of the sounds in words tended to make 'bad' errors and made little progress. By tracking the development of phonological awareness, letter knowledge and error type, Stuart and Coltheart showed that, when the children became phonologically aware and knew at least 13 letters, the balance of their errors changed from being predominantly types 1, 2 and 3 to being predominantly types 4 and 5. Types 4 and 5 errors are evidence of using a sublexical route to working out words and Stuart and Coltheart's study showed that this is a necessary development if children are to progress in reading.

It seems reasonable that knowledge of letters should be a prerequisite for using a sublexical route to reading. Adams (1990) has reported that knowledge of letters was the single best predictor of reading performance. However, in order to map the letters onto sounds, you also need to be aware of the sound structure of the words: there is no point in having just one part of the puzzle. Stuart and Coltheart clearly showed that phonological awareness was also an important determinant. This is not a unique finding in the psychology of reading literature. Indeed there is overwhelming evidence that those children who are phonologically aware and have a knowledge of the letters of the alphabet at an early age go on to be better readers and spellers and find is easier to learn to read (Gough, Juel and Griffiths, 1992; Wagner and Torgesen, 1987).

What is phonological awareness? There is a problem in interpreting the literature because there is no agreed definition and so different researchers will use slightly different tests to study it. However, for the purposes of this chapter it will be defined as the ability to reflect upon the sound structure of words and to manipulate those sounds. A simple level of phonological awareness would be the ability to recognise when two words rhyme while a more complex level would involve insights about alliteration. More sophisticated phonological awareness is involved for adding or deleting specified sounds in words and a further refinement would be blending and segmenting sounds and words. The precise level of phonological awareness which is optimally effective for efficient reading development has yet to be mapped. In a study of children who were fluent readers before they began school we have found very large differences in all aspects of phonological awareness between the young early readers and a matched control group of non-readers who were the same age, same sex, same socio-economic background, entering the same school class at the same time and who had the same level of vocabulary development (Stainthorp and Hughes, 1995).

A seminal study by Bradley and Bryant (1983) showed that children who were better at rhyming and alliteration identification in nursery school went on to be better readers and spellers when they began to learn to read in the primary school. This advantage was maintained. When this phonological awareness was linked with knowledge of letters there was an impressive advantage. It was this study that encouraged so much investigation into the effects of phonological awareness on reading performance.

Research and effective practice

So far then we have considered research evidence showing that children who have knowledge of letters and who are phonologically aware pre-school and in the early years of Key Stage 1 go on to be better readers and spellers. What we need to know is whether or not this is a simple, stable individual difference between children or whether it is possible to intervene at an early stage to teach children to be phonologically aware so that they are prepared to make use of letter-sound knowledge when they begin to learn to read. There is evidence relevant to this from training studies.

Bryant and Bradley (1985) showed that children who were not phonologically aware in the nursery schools could be taught to rhyme and do alliteration in Key Stage 1 and that this had a beneficial, though modest, effect on their reading and spelling performance. Children who were taught about letters as well did considerably better.

Lundberg, Frost and Petersen (1988) published the results of a more extensive training programme in Denmark involving 235 pre-school six year olds and 155 control children. The training programme was designed to take place over a period of eight months with daily sessions of 15 to 20 minutes in groups of between 15 and 20. The programme systematically worked through all aspects of phonological awareness. Different aspects were gradually built into the daily activities, but the children were always given opportunities for playing games to ensure consolidation of earlier learning. None of the activities would be considered unusual or even novel in a nursery school. The whole programme was based on games, including singing and dancing and playing with language. Some pictorial materials were used, but no letters as it was a deliberate policy of kindergarten schools in Denmark to avoid any instruction of reading or pre-reading.

All the children – both training and control groups – were tested on various measures before the start of the programme to ensure equivalence of the groups at the start of the study. Tests included pre-reading ability, letter knowledge, language comprehension for following directions, vocabulary and phonological knowledge. These tests were repeated nine months later, after the training programme had ended. One important finding was that the children who had received the phonological training showed significantly greater improvement than the control children on the tests of phonological knowledge. This meant that it had been possible to teach children to become aware of the sound structure of the language. When they further analysed performance on the phonological tests, they found that the area which showed the greatest level of improvement was that of phoneme awareness.

The children's subsequent reading and spelling performance was tested when they were in Grade 1 and again in Grade 2. This was the acid test of the phonological training programme as there is no point in teaching children to be phonologically aware if it has no enduring beneficial effect on literacy. The results showed that the Training Group only had a marginal advantage in reading at Grade 1 but a significant advantage by Grade 2. When spelling was assessed, this advantage was even clearer as the Training Group did significantly better in both Grade 1 and Grade 2. Further analysis showed that children's ability to manipulate phonemes before they started reading instruction was a powerful predictor of reading and spelling performance in Grades 1 and 2. This training study confirms that phonological awareness is an important predictor of literacy development, that it is possible to teach children to become aware of the phonemes and, therefore, that it is possible to affect the ease with which they will subsequently be able to learn to read and spell.

Byrne and Fielding-Barnsley (1991) published a training programme which aims to develop phonological awareness in which children are introduced to a small subset of sounds for which they receive intensive teaching. This teaching is designed to start the process of becoming aware of the sounds in words with the idea that when children have mastered the phonemic principle, they will be able to generalise their knowledge to all the sounds in the language. Unlike many research studies, this programme was related specifically to a set of materials that were designed as teaching resources. The programme is designed around a set of Key Sounds: 7 consonant sounds / s /, / m /, / p /, / g /, / l /, / t /, / sh /; and 2 vowel sounds / a / and / e /. Children first become aware of a consonant sound as a beginning sound and then as an end sound. The vowels are just used as beginning sounds. Though the programme can be worked without reference to letters, they found that the teaching was more effective if the children's alphabet knowledge was linked to their increasing understanding of the phonemic principle. The teaching programme is designed to last just twelve weeks with the rationale that once the children have been taught about alliteration and ending sounds, that knowledge will be of use when they learn to read.

Byrne and Fielding-Barnsley (1993) found that children who had taken part in the programme began their primary school with a head start as far as reading and spelling were concerned. This confirms the findings of Lundberg, Frost and Petersen (1988) that it is possible to teach children in groups about the sound structure of words. In giving children this knowledge, they are able to utilise it when they come to try to crack the alphabetic code in reading and spelling. Byrne and Fielding-Barnsley confirmed that it was level of phonological awareness *per se* which tended to predict performance in reading and spelling. Some of the children in their control group who had not received any specific phonological awareness training, nevertheless did develop it by the time they entered primary school. These children also had an advantage in reading and spelling. The case that Byrne and Fielding-Barnsley wish to make is that the programme increased the proportion of children '...achieving and maintaining the critical insights into phonological structure' (1993, p109). As yet there is no way of predicting which children are likely to develop phonological awareness spontaneously through their everyday experiences, so it is probably more effective to err on the side of caution and play phonological games with everyone. It will not harm the children who are naturally phonologically aware and it will give those who are not that extra boost. It will also ensure that Year R teachers are alerted to the children who seem to have the greatest difficulty developing these insights.

The Reading Recovery programme discussed in Chapter 8 has now been well researched as a means of helping individual children who are having difficulties. This has been built up using methods that were effective, but not specifically grounded in any theoretical framework. Hatcher, Hulme and Ellis (1994) conducted an extensive research programme, one aim of which was to develop effective 'booster' teaching, for those children who had failed to become fluent readers by the time they were six to seven year olds. They showed that, following training to develop phonological awareness which was then *explicitly* linked with a reading programme similar to Reading Recovery, children made significantly accelerated progress in reading and spelling. Hatcher et al. point out that spending the same amount of time on developing phonological awareness at this stage was of little use. Listening to the children reading books without explicitly giving them the skills for working out the words was useful, but not as good as giving a combination of phonology linked to reading. This confirmed the findings of Byrne and Fielding-Barnsley, that developing children's phonological awareness and enabling them to use this knowledge to map sounds onto letters gives them a strategy for decoding written words into component sounds and thereby using a sublexical route to word identification.

The three programmes discussed above explicitly teach children to become aware of the phonemic nature of words and yet the aspect of phonological awareness which seems easiest for children to achieve is found to be at the level of rhyme and alliteration. There is no 'real life' reason why children should be consciously aware of the phonemic nature of language except that it seems to help in learning to read in an alphabetic script. There is, however, a considerable body of work that shows that the segmenting of words into *onset* and *rime* has a great deal of validity for children (Treiman, 1985, 1992). In developing phonological awareness, sensitivity to rhyme (and thereby alliteration) may have primacy.

The onset of a word is the initial consonant sound or consonant cluster. The rime is the final vowel or vowel plus consonant(s). Thus, in a word such as BIN, made up of the three sounds / b / + / i / + / n /, the / b / sound is the onset and the / i / + / n / is the rime. When two words rhyme they share the same rime. Goswami (1986, 1988) has shown that it is possible to capitalise on this when teaching children to read. When children have gained letter-sound knowledge, they can begin to use both elements of decoding and analogy to read new words successfully. Children taught to read a word like BEAK could map the B onto the onset and the EAK onto the rime. This enabled them to use analogical skills to recognise the similarity between BEAK and new words like PEAK and LEAK. This strategy seems to capitalise on lexical and sublexical procedures. Kirtley (1995) has developed a set of card games which are specifically designed to build up the use of rhyme and analogy when recognising words. Analogy is another way of ensuring that phonic knowledge is used generatively to work out unknown words when reading text.

Good practice and effective practice

As we saw earlier, the major shift in HMI recommendations for 'good practice' in the teaching of reading occurred with no explanation or serious argument. A review of the evidence from psychological research on reading provides support for the most recent of the HMI claims. This research leads us to expect that the most effective teachers will be those who teach systematic phonics and link this directly to reading and other literacy activities including compositional writing, handwriting and spelling. Phonological awareness plus letter knowledge provides children with a framework which enables them to develop the sublexical route to reading which in turn ensures that they can begin to become independent readers. It means they can develop a strategy whereby they can achieve success. Success is itself motivating. This means that children who find it easy to begin reading are likely to read more. The more they read, the easier it becomes because they are developing their word reading skills to the point where they become automatic. This means that children can get on an upward spiral.

Not all children will be able to develop insights about the alphabetic nature of written English unaided. Those who do not will find reading a difficult activity. Because it is difficult, they tend to read much more slowly, process far fewer words and read far less frequently than skilled readers. This means that they have less opportunity to develop their skill, so it remains difficult. They read less and they make far less progress. This has been called the 'Matthew Effect' by Stanovich (1986) who suggested that initial advantages in reading acquisition have strong feedback effects on other reading-related activities. He has shown that exposure to print has a significant effect on reading development (Stanovich and West, 1989; Stanovich and Cunningham, 1992; West and Stanovich, 1991). However, Stanovich makes it clear that children need to develop the sublexical route for reading words in order to develop sufficient skill to be able to read independently. Teachers cannot afford to take chances. They need to ensure that all children are phonologically aware and have a letter-sound knowledge that they can apply. Some children hardly need any teaching in this area at all. Others need considerable help.

If we piece together the empirical evidence about the relationship between early phonological awareness and reading development; the relationship between letter knowledge and reading development; the use of analogy for building up words; the positive, beneficial effect of linking phonological awareness directly to reading activities; and the effect of exposure to print on the development of mastery, we begin to develop a strong body of evidence on the teaching of reading. This suggests clearly HMI's most recent pronouncements on 'good practice' are in line with evidence for effective practice in a way that was not true of the earlier recommendations.

Because reading is an activity which does not develop automatically through living in human society, children have to be given explicit instruction. The evidence from experimental psychology is that (a) children need to develop an explicit awareness of the sound structure of the language in order to map the sounds onto letters and (b) those children who have this knowledge find it easier to learn to read. This knowledge enables them to build a sublexical route to reading which in turn enables them to tackle any unknown word with a degree of success. The more they do this, the easier word reading becomes because they build up orthographic identities which enable them to access the words directly. When children are given teaching to develop their phonological awareness and letter knowledge which ensures that they use this knowledge to good effect when reading a wide range of materials, then they make good progress. The evidence from psychological experiments and HMI's more recent reports about effective teaching of reading dovetail beautifully. Teachers now have a sound theoretical and empirical explanation for why current thinking on 'good practice' provides a basis for effective teaching.

CHAPTER 8
Special Educational Needs

Diana Moses

Definitions and incidence

Much of the debate in the field of special educational needs since the mid 1970s has centred around definitions and the subsequent proportion of pupils who are defined as having special needs. It is inappropriate to deal in detail with these matters here but it is important to begin with an outline of these background concerns together with the highlighting of some of the most significant issues.

There is no universally agreed definition of special educational need and consequently no absolute and indisputable number of children to whom the description of having special educational needs applies. Nevertheless, approximately the same numbers have been estimated using quite different methods of enquiry. The epidemiological study of learning difficulties conducted on the Isle of Wight (Rutter, Tizard and Whitmore, 1970), whose findings were used as the main basis for the Warnock Committee's definitions and recommendations, came to very similar conclusions to Croll and Moses's (1985) survey of teachers' perceptions of special needs. Rutter et al. concluded that about 20 per cent of pupils experience some sort of special educational need and Croll and Moses found that primary school teachers regarded approximately 18 per cent as having special needs. The similarity of the results of these two very different types of survey indicates a substantial consensus on a working definition and overall incidence of special needs in the English education system. Nevertheless there is still some variation between schools and between LEAs and this is a matter of some concern. In 1992 both Lady Warnock and the Audit Commission expressed dissatisfaction with how LEAs were administering the 1981 Act and were particularly worried about the variation that existed across the country, especially for pupils in ordinary schools with less severe special needs.

Despite the changes in terminology introduced by the 1981 Act and the concurrent changes in thinking about 'handicap' and special needs, distinctions remain between the approximately two per cent of pupils for whom education in a special school may be considered and the 18 per cent of pupils who also have special educational needs but of a less acute kind. These differences are reflected in the research. There is a considerable body of research on ways of teaching pupils with sensory impairments, physical disabilities, autism and other profound and serious handicaps which will remain the subject of specialist expertise but never, in a routine way, form part of all primary teachers' skills. However, research which addresses the issues of integration is of relevance to primary teachers.

Research investigating the learning difficulties of the 18 per cent of pupils in mainstream schools tends to be less specialist in nature and many studies of classroom learning which are not specifically directed towards learning difficulties still have implications for the teaching of pupils with special needs. It is with these pupils and with this type of research that this chapter is mainly, but not exclusively, concerned.

Integration

One of the key requirements of the 1981 Act, based on a recommendation of the Warnock Report, was for all children to be educated together in mainstream schools, i.e. 'handicapped' children should be integrated into ordinary schools. The foundation underlying the move towards integration is philosophical rather than pragmatic and these different approaches are reflected in the different types of research undertaken. There is extensive literature on comparisons of performance of pupils attending special schools and ordinary schools. Much of this work was conducted in the USA and has been reviewed by Epps and Tindal (1987). Although these studies are by no means identical they do tend to belong to the same tradition of research and work with the same basic methodology. They are centrally concerned with the effectiveness of different types of provision and seek measurable outcomes to establish the superiority of one type of provision over another. However, in contrasting children's performance in ordinary and special schools this approach has not yielded definitive answers. Typically the studies have been small-scale quasi-experiments comparing one group of pupils in an ordinary school with another group, matched as far as possible, to a group in a special school or schools. The more rigorously conducted of these studies do indeed establish, within the parameters of the enquiry, which educational setting resulted in superior pupil performance and this finding may have had considerable impact on provision in the schools in which the research was conducted. However, meta-analyses of a considerable number of these studies do not confirm the superiority of one type of provision over another. The majority of these type of studies were conducted in the 1970s but there are current examples of this type of approach (Martlew and Hodson, 1991) and, as long as their findings are considered sensibly and not dismissed because they do not provide definitive answers to big questions, they can add to our understanding of providing for children with special educational needs.

The lack of a definitive answer to the issue of type of school had a major impact on the sort of research conducted into integration. Research did not firmly establish that segregated schooling provided pupils with a 'special' education that was unavailable elsewhere and concurrently the climate of thought in education also shifted. Influenced in the UK by notions of the extension of the comprehensivisation of education to include all children and in the US by Civil Rights concepts of entitlement, the ideology of the desirability and the morality of integration became established in educational thinking. This ideological position had a profound effect on much of the subsequent research carried out on integration issues. The most widely known of these studies was carried out by Hegarty and Pocklington and reported in *Educating Pupils with Special Needs in the Ordinary School* (1981) and *Integration in Action* (1982).

Hegarty and Pocklington started out, not with the neutral, impartial stance traditionally regarded as appropriate for social researchers but with a commitment to the moral superiority and desirability of integrated provision. For them the research question was not 'which type of provision is the most effective?' but 'how can we demonstrate that integration can work?' This second question is not of the same magnitude as the first and is not as difficult to answer. Their position is made quite explicit; 'The starting point was the presence of pupils with special needs in ordinary schools. *Given this presumption in favour of integration...*' and also, 'As long as some pupils attend special schools when their peers with comparable special needs elsewhere receive satisfactory education in ordinary schools, *there are grounds for disquiet*' (my italics) (Hegarty and Pocklington, 1981, p507). Through a number of case studies Hegarty and Pocklington demonstrate through detailed description and analysis how pupils with a wide range of special educational needs were being integrated into a number of schools using a variety of strategies. This work does show that pupils with a wide range of special education needs – those suffering from physical disabilities, sensory impairment, moderate and severe learning difficulties and behavioural problems – can all be accommodated in some sort of integration programme in mainstream schools. The fact that these examples exist is in itself proof that all children, irrespective of special needs, can be educated together.

Using the same methodology, Hodgson, Clunies-Ross and Hegarty

(1984) followed up this work with a closer look at actual classroom practice and identified factors in curriculum and teaching style which they regarded as contributing to 'successful' practice. But the success of these various integration programmes is not judged in terms of any sort of measurable outcomes for the pupils concerned, but is based on the researchers' observations and the expressed opinions of those professionals, parents and pupils who were participating in the scheme. This approach to evaluation will be returned to later in the chapter.

It can be argued that this is the type of research that is of practical help, but this is only true if this is based on a prior commitment to integration. It certainly gave considerable encouragement to those seeking to implement integration policies and presented guidelines which could be used to assist in this process. On the other hand, it can be argued that the case study approach used and the prior commitment to integration means that the results obtained are really of limited significance. If a study using similar methodology had started off with an ideological commitment to education in special schools then, through conducting case studies of schools where professionals, parents and pupils were enthusiastic about segregated provision (and such schools could easily have been found), the conclusion drawn would have been that special schooling does work and, similarly, guidelines to assist in successful implementation could have been produced.

However, the studies comparing special and ordinary schooling, especially when they are all considered together, also present problems. The meta-analysis of these studies, often very competent individual pieces of work, suggest that the measurable differences in pupil characteristics including academic performance, behaviour, social adjustment and attitudes did not depend directly upon where pupils were educated. An assumption that something 'special' always happened in special schools is clearly not justified but neither is the notion that ordinary schools can necessarily do as well or better.

Croll and Moses (1985) found that, overall, primary school teachers are in favour of integrating pupils with all types of special education needs into the mainstream school. Teachers would appear to be most favourably disposed towards including pupils with sensory impairment and physical disabilities and more apprehensive about being able to cope well with pupils with learning and behaviour problems. Across all types of difficulty teachers are more favourably disposed towards the inclusion of children with the sort of difficulties they have met before. This finding is encouraging for teachers, other professionals and parents as it suggests that initial reluctance to include a child who might otherwise be placed in a special school is likely to disappear as the result of experience.

Special educational needs in the primary classroom

Overall, the vast majority of pupils with special needs are in ordinary schools and, in the primary school, whatever the exact nature of the arrangements made to meet special needs, the class teacher will be of prime importance. The study of special educational needs in primary schools conducted by Croll and Moses (1985) provides considerable information about teachers, pupils, policy, provision and practice and although it does not include a detailed exploration of pedagogy its findings do have major pedagogical implications.

This study found that teachers' main concerns are with learning problems and particularly with reading problems; 13.5 per cent of the total sample of over 12,000 pupils were considered to have a reading problem; about four pupils in the average classroom.

The 428 primary teachers involved in this study were of the opinion that 18.8 per cent of the pupils in their classes had special educational needs; that is between 5 and 6 children in an average class of 29 or 30. By far the largest group were pupils with learning difficulties; just over 16 per cent of the whole sample of 12,310 pupils. Roughly half this figure (nearly 8 per cent) had behaviour problems and just over 4 per cent of pupils had either sensory impairments, physical disabilities or health problems. There was overlap between these categories especially between learning difficulties and behaviour problems, approximately 5 per cent of the whole sample had both learning difficulties and behaviour problems, that is well over a quarter of all pupils with special needs. There is undoubtedly a connection between learning and behaviour problems but this study, together with most other research conducted in this area, does not disentangle cause and effect. 'Do pupils display behavioural difficulties in the classroom because they are experiencing difficulties with learning or do children, at least in part, develop difficulties because of their behaviour?' There is no straightforward answer to this question and, almost certainly, the relationship between behaviour and learning is both complex and varies between individual children.

Over the full range of special needs the ratio of boys to girls among the nominated pupils was almost two to one, a result similar to the findings of epidemiological studies of such difficulties (Rutter, Tizard and Whitmore, 1970; Pringle, Butler and Davey, 1966). Learning difficulties were attributed to 19.5 per cent of boys and 11.1 per cent of girls, behavioural difficulties to 10.9 per cent of boys and 4.5 per cent of girls and health and related problems to 5.8 per cent of boys and 2.9 per cent of girls. The most dramatic difference is in the category of discipline problems, where boys outnumber girls by almost four to one. Overall, 24.4 per cent of boys were described as having special educational needs compared with 13.2 per cent of girls.

Just as learning difficulties dominate the teacher's view of special needs, so reading problems are regarded as the major element of learning difficulties. Almost nine out of ten children with learning difficulties were described by their teachers as poor readers. These children make up 13.5 per cent of the total sample, about four pupils in an average classroom. A comparison of reading test scores, teacher assessments and other variables suggests that certain other characteristics of pupils and classrooms may influence teacher assessments. At particular levels of reading ability, boys were more likely than girls, children with behaviour problems rather than pupils without them and younger children within a class were more likely than older children to be identified as poor readers. In addition, children in classes where the overall level of performance is high are more likely to be identified as poor readers than children with the same level of difficulty who are in classes where the overall standard is lower.

This suggests that assessment could be improved and the introduction of the Code of Practice may assist in this (DfE, 1994). The consequences of variation in assessments are not clear-cut and are open to a variety of interpretations. For example if a child in a regular classroom is a non-reader or virtual non-reader at 8 or 9 years then for this situation to go undetected and for the child consequently to receive no help would be a disaster. On the other hand, for a child with only slightly below average reading performance in a class where the general level is particularly high to be regarded as a poor reader is potentially problematic. Teacher knowledge of possible factors that may affect their assessments can improve practice and, in this instance, alert teachers to the potential pitfalls of overlooking the difficulties of girls and older pupils in their classes and of underestimating the level of performance of boys and children with behaviour problems.

Systematic classroom observation established that, overall, pupils with learning or behaviour problems spent less time engaged in work than other pupils but that different types of classroom organisation had a greater effect on these children than on the rest of the class. Engagement in work was higher during group than class lessons and much higher than during individual work. While the type of work organisation is associated with only small differences in levels of engagement for the majority of children in the class, for children with learning or behavioural difficulties whose overall level of engagement is below average, the type of work organisation is associated with considerable differences in involvement. This finding strongly suggests that some forms of group work have the potential to be particularly effective for pupils with special educational needs.

Teachers spend more time with both children with learning difficulties and with behaviour problems than they do with other members of the class but, inevitably this still amounts to only a very small proportion of the school day. In a typical primary classroom where the emphasis is on individual work the teacher will spend the majority of the day interacting with individual children but the children will spend most of their time working on their own with only brief spells of individual contact with the teacher. Children with learning difficulties receive private individual attention for 3.3 per cent of the time and children with behaviour problems for 3.2 per cent of the time, compared with 1.9 per cent for other pupils. If all individual attention is counted, including individual attention in the context of groups and the whole class, both these figures rise to 4.1 per cent, contrasted with 2.5 per cent for the others. The two most important points here are that teachers are prepared to give a larger share of their time to pupils with problems but, in the context of classroom organisation based mainly on individual work, this time will inevitably be limited.

The National Curriculum and special educational needs

The reactions among teachers and educationalists to the effects of the National Curriculum on the education of children with learning difficulties have been very varied and the longer-term consequences are still not at all clear. The National Curriculum Council document on special educational needs, *A Curriculum for All* (NCC, 1989) emphasised the entitlement of all pupils to a broad and balanced curriculum. It was the clear intention of the NCC and the DfE that the National Curriculum should be followed by all pupils with the possible exception of a small number of pupils for whom schools would have to apply for exemptions. On the one hand, the entitlement to a common curriculum held out the promise of a wider curriculum experience for children with learning difficulties and a reduction in the marginalisation of such children. On the other hand, it was feared that the emphasis on assessment both for individual pupils and indirectly for schools together with a 'back to basics' tendency would actually result in a further narrowing of the curriculum for pupils with learning difficulties and in teachers having less time for these children as they were forced to concentrate more on whole class teaching and focusing on class average levels of achievement.

The PACE study suggests that the relative amount of individual contact between teachers and pupils with learning difficulties compared with other class members has declined since the Croll and Moses study and also that 'the continued heavy emphasis on the basic subjects in the primary curriculum following the introduction of the National Curriculum has been experienced even more strongly by children regarded by their teachers as low achievers than by other children' (Croll, 1996). There is general agreement that it is regrettable if teachers are spending less time with pupils with learning difficulties but the increased emphasis on basic subjects reopens a debate over curriculum for slow learners that has a long history. In essence this debate is over the extent to which pupils with learning difficulties should spend their time acquiring basic skills as opposed to experiencing a broader curriculum which is not heavily based on those basic skills (Brennan, 1974).

Currently, in addition to the National Curriculum resulting in increased emphasis on the basic subjects, the introduction of Individual Educational Programmes(IEPs) under the Code of Practice will probably, but not inevitably, also result in increased differentiation and concentration on the basics for pupils with learning difficulties. Dyson, Millward and Skidmore echo concerns expressed by Hart (1992) and Thompson and Barton (1992) that 'such individualisation may simply replace the structural segregation of learners by a segregation based on individuals working at ever more subtly differentiated levels of the curriculum' (Dyson et al., 1994, p311).

A recent report commissioned by the DfE, *Innovatory Practice in Mainstream Schools* (Clark et al., 1995), sought to identify and document practice in schools which the schools themselves and their LEAs regarded as innovative. Practices were found to be very varied but it was also claimed that broad similarities emerged:

> At the heart of the approach is a commitment to locate provision for all pupils firmly in the mainstream class and to develop a repertoire of strategies which will ensure that access to an entitlement curriculum, thereby responding to a wider range of pupil diversity. Central to this endeavour are four key principles: The creative deployment of resources to support the learning of all pupils: the development of the school as an organisation able to respond to diversity: enhancement of the professional skills of all staff as the key agents of learning, and, providing a culture of collaborative support for staff and students by drawing on the widest possible resource base. (p3)

It is interesting that these practices should be regarded as particularly innovative in the 1990s. There is probably a wide consensus on the desirability of these developments but as innovations their beginnings go back to the early 1980s, if not before. Probably the most recently innovative aspect of these developments is the production by the schools of detailed documentation concerning their policy and practice so that what they are actually doing is more apparent and more open to discussion and debate within and outside the school.

The approaches to teaching children with learning difficulties varied considerably between the schools which were all regarded as moving in the same 'innovative' directions. Together with most studies of this general type there was no attempt at evaluation; this is made quite explicit in the report: 'Our intention...was not so much to evaluate the quality or outcomes of schools' work, but to understand as fully as possible the approaches they were taking to special needs and their reasons for developing this response' (Clark et al., 1995, p8).

This seeming reluctance to undertake evaluation is understandable. With our current level of theoretical knowledge about the basic cognitive processes, about how we learn things, and the range of conflicting theories (and notions that are not substantial enough to be called theories) about children's classroom learning, it is going to be virtually impossible to establish a 'best' way of teaching. Because definitive proof of the superiority of one particular approach may not be possible, it is tempting to think that all approaches are equally valid and equally productive and to abandon attempts to 'prove' and explain success. There may not be one best way but there are a number of better ways.

An objectives approach

Much has been written over the last twenty years about the nature of learning difficulties, their real and perceived origins and the best way to alleviate them. The differences between those advocating different types of approaches are essentially differences in ideology rather than a dispute over effectiveness. Diane Montgomery, for example, advocates an attempt 'to transform teaching from the content-based, expository approaches to which pupils *have been subjected* to cognitive process methodology suitable for pupils learning' (my italics, note the emotive terminology). She wants to emphasise the desirability of 'training pupils to learn how to learn' and talks about a 'process' emphasis in the teaching model. The purpose of education is described in terms of helping pupils to think efficiently and then to communicate their thoughts. (Montgomery, 1990, p123.) This approach and an objectives approach represent different ways of looking at learning and teaching in general and are not limited to learning difficulties.

As has been demonstrated in other chapters, an objectives approach to classroom learning and behaviour has much to recommend it and there are many examples of this approach to learning difficulties resulting in success. Nevertheless there is considerable reluctance both on the part of many teachers and educationalists to accept this situation. There appears to be a very poorly reasoned but very strong antipathy to what is seen as mechanistic and authoritarian. Wheldall and Congreve (1981) reported that class teachers knew very little about behavioural approaches to teaching and neither the underlying psychological theory nor the techniques built upon the theory had been part of their professional training. However when they learned more about behavioural approaches and how to apply them they became enthusiastic. It is significant that even educationalists who, in most respects, are strongly opposed to an objectives approach recognise its value in relation to the acquisition of basic skills for those experiencing learning difficulties. (Montgomery, 1990.)

An objectives approach to teaching and learning is associated with four activities – assessment through teaching, setting behavioural objectives, precision teaching and direct instruction, but in any particular intervention programme they do not all have to be present together. Assessment through teaching emphasises the importance of determining exactly what a child can and cannot do, constructing a programme to meet the individual child's needs and continuously assessing progress and modifying teaching. Behavioural objectives provide the 'building blocks' of instructional materials (Leadbetter and Winteringham, 1986). It is very important to make a clear statement of what pupil behaviour the teaching is designed to achieve. Behavioural objectives do not necessarily have to be decided solely by the teacher and then 'imposed' upon the child. Depending on the individual circumstances, it is possible for teacher and pupil to negotiate and collaborate on objectives. An objectives approach to teaching and learning is just as open to collaborative working and the pupil taking part in decision-making as any other approach. One of the great advantages of setting objectives is 'seeing' them realised and being able to show evidence of real success.

Precision teaching is a technique which enables teachers to measure small changes in a pupil's performance each day and so keep a careful eye on progress. It also encourages a considerable amount of over-learning which facilitates mastery. Precision teaching is essentially a particular framework within which learning is organised and recorded; it does not in itself constitute a teaching style (Formentin and Csapo, 1980). Direct instruction involves explicitly teaching the pupil the knowledge and skills directly relevant to reaching the objective. In the case of basic skills, pupils will be taught specific numeracy and literacy skills. Preparing children by 'improving self-esteem' or by developing sensory-motor skills, for example, play no part in direct instruction.

DISTAR is a well-known example of a direct instruction programme which consists of a sequence of scripted lessons and homework assignments which was developed as part of the Headstart Programme (Englemann and Carnine, 1982; Carnine and Gilbert, 1979). The whole of the Headstart programme has been the subject of successive evaluations over the years and both its immediate impact and, even more importantly, its long-term effects, now seen beyond doubt. Nevertheless DISTAR has not proved popular with teachers in English schools (Pearson and Lindsay, 1986) but an English development, DATAPAC, is more widely used (Leadbetter and Winteringham, 1986).

DATAPAC, or Daily Teaching and Assessment for Primary Aged Children, is a direct instruction package of materials aimed at children who are experiencing difficulties in acquiring the basic skills of maths, handwriting, spelling and reading. Both the procedures recommended and the teaching materials would fit in well with the new requirement of IEPs for pupils with special needs. Unlike DISTAR, DATAPAC is not prescriptive and is flexible enough to incorporate modifications that teachers might wish to make. Because of the underlying principles and the procedures used, teachers and pupils using DATAPAC and similar approaches can see how well it is working. In this way it is, in a sense, undergoing continuous evaluation. Another type of evaluation established that over 80 per cent of 150 teachers who had used DATAPAC and had replied to the evaluation questionnaire responded that they were 'very impressed' with the package (Leadbetter and Winteringham, 1986). This finding clearly indicates a high level of teacher satisfaction but the scope of the evaluation was limited. There was no attempt to establish onward measures of improvement in pupil performance, neither was there any attempt to compare that particular package either with similar materials or with other types of approaches.

Measuring effectiveness

Comparisons between the effectiveness of different types of interventions are rare and are fraught with difficulty but Somerville and Leach (1988) carried out such an evaluation with extremely interesting and significant results. They compared the effectiveness of three different types of intervention programmes on the specific reading difficulties of forty 10 and 11 years olds. The children were randomly assigned to one of three intervention programmes or a control group. Group 1 participated in a **psycho-motor** programme composed of a wide variety of relevant exercises. Group 2 followed a **self-esteem** programme and Group 3, those on the **direct instruction** programme, were placed on the Corrective Reading Programme (Engelmann, Hanner and Haddox, 1980) which is a fully scripted, task-analysed reading programme which is based on well-developed direct instruction principals (Engelmann and Carnine, 1982). All programmes involved the same amount of participatory time and each involved homework tasks and the participation of parents. (It is interesting to note that the first author of this report had been in the practice of using mainly psycho-motor programme interventions.) After a period of 12 weeks the direct instruction group had made very significant progress with their reading whereas the psycho-motor group and the self-esteem group had progressed no better than the control group with reading skills and, significantly, had not improved in terms of psycho-motor skills or self-esteem. The numbers are small and the gains were measured only immediately after the completion of the programme but, nevertheless, the results are impressive.

This work is unusual in that it compares programmes representing three different types of intervention but, as the authors point out, it is not unusual in demonstrating the effectiveness of direct instruction. Another aspect of this evaluation does go some way to explaining a resistance to direct instruction in spite of its success. As well as measuring reading skills the researchers also asked students, teachers and parents which programme they perceived as being successful and which they had enjoyed most. All three experimental programmes were perceived as being equally successful at improving reading skills but the other programmes were regarded as more enjoyable and the teachers perceived the self-esteem programme as having the greatest positive effect on general classroom performance. Secondly, analysis of individual responses to the programmes showed that although, overall, the indirect programmes did not enjoy a high degree of success, they did nevertheless result in considerable improvement for a few individuals. The conclusion drawn from the data is that:

> Taken in conjunction with the more positive subjective reactions generally to psycho-motor and self-esteem programmes, these data support the view that such programmes may be maintained in practice by reinforcement from positive consumer feedback and by occasional individual success. (Somerville and Leach, 1988, pp51–2)

This conclusion needs to be kept in mind when teachers are choosing intervention programmes and when they or researchers are seeking to evaluate programmes. Individual successes and the enjoyment of participants in the programmes are both highly desirable but not necessarily associated with the most effective programmes. What direct instruction can take from other methods is the importance of learning being enjoyable. The challenge is to make direct instruction fun and there would seem to be no reason why this cannot be done.

Another intervention programme that has received a great deal of attention in recent years and has been the subject of numerous evaluations is Reading Recovery (Clay, 1979, 1985, 1993). This programme was devised by Marie Clay for use in New Zealand but it has now been introduced into parts of the United States, Canada and Australia and in a more limited way into the United Kingdom. In New Zealand, Reading Recovery is a national programme which provides individual help for pupils who are falling behind in their reading after one year of schooling. It is particularly important to note that, although the intervention is directly targeted at individual children, it was intended for use within an educational system that places great emphasis on securing initial literacy. This is evident particularly in the amount of time devoted to reading and associated skills both in the primary classroom and in the training of teachers, and in 'the structural approaches to the teaching of initial reading which were recognisable in all the primary schools visited' (OFSTED, 1993a, p4).

The strategy of the Reading Recovery programme is to offer additional help to pupils who are failing to become independent readers after one year's instruction. Usually the children selected are those who are performing poorly in relation to the rest of their class. It is explicitly aimed at individual poor readers and is not a method of raising generally low standards. Pupils on the programme are withdrawn from their classrooms for half an hour a day each day for intensive one-to-one tuition with a specially trained Reading Recovery teacher. The essential feature of the intervention is that it is both highly structured and is closely differentiated, according to the needs of the individual child.

The approach adopted towards reading is one in which both meaning and the full range of analytical and decoding strategies, including phonic cueing are taught. Writing, spelling, speaking and listening skills are also integrated into the work on reading and form a part of every lesson. The OFSTED report on Reading Recovery in New Zealand also claims that pupils whose reading improves are also often reported to be making additional gains in confidence, school attendance and in other subjects including mathematics (OFSTED, 1993a). This claim is interesting as it reverses the more frequent assertion that improved self-esteem is a prerequisite for improved academic performance. It is also based on the type of reported evidence that Somerville and Leach have demonstrated to be unreliable, as has been previously discussed.

Nevertheless, although evaluations differ about exactly how effective Reading Recovery is, they all agree that it is an effective way to raise the performance of poor readers. As already stated, the programme involves the withdrawal of individual children from the classroom but there is reason to believe that this procedure is decreasingly popular in UK schools. The Croll and Moses survey indicated that in the early 1980s withdrawal for extra help with reading was both widespread and popular among teachers, but more recently Clarke et al. in their work on innovatory practice claim that, although many schools continue to withdraw children, there was also a sense that withdrawal was a 'last resort' (Clarke et al., 1995).

Evaluations carried out in Australia have highlighted some of the difficulties both in the actual implementation of Reading Recovery in schools in a different educational system and additional difficulties in the evaluation. Nevertheless the overall conclusions from rigorous evaluations are that Reading Recovery is successfully transferable to different educational systems (Wheldall, Center and Freeman, 1993). There are also some indications that it would be even more successful if the initial teaching of reading was more similar to that used in New Zealand. Center et al. conclude their study of implementation in New South Wales by saying 'these results do add to the growing literature on the need to develop instructional programmes in phonological awareness, phonological recording and syntactic awareness in the very early years of schooling' (Center et al., 1995, pp260–1). This is the same approach to the initial teaching of reading as was described in Chapter 7.

Over the last twenty years research in the field of special needs has been very varied. One type of research has concentrated on increasing our knowledge of various handicapping conditions and developing strategies to maximise the learning of children with disabilities. In contrast, a substantial proportion of research activity has been directed towards issues of policy and provision and while this sort of research may have implications for classroom practice, it does not have pedagogy as a central concern. Many aspects of special needs education are the subject of philosophical debate and ideological commitment, particularly to integration, and this has determined the nature of some of the research undertaken. Similarly, special needs education is subject to the same debates and controversies as the rest of the education system; in most respects special needs education is not a world apart.

This chapter has looked at various types of special needs research and evaluations of various programmes and considered the significance of findings and their implications for teaching. One of the main conclusions to be drawn is the strength of the objectives approach. Even if there is currently opposition to its more general use, the research evidence suggests that an objectives approach to the teaching of basic skills to children experiencing difficulties is genuinely effective and teachers need to be very sure of alternative methods before they reject this approach.

Research has also established that there can be a difference between the perception of success and real success and that this confusion is associated with the experience of undertaking the programme. It would appear that objectives approaches can be dull, even if they are, in fact, best at enhancing performance. The teaching challenge is to take the proven success of an objectives approach and to make it fun for children.

CHAPTER 9

Differentiation? Working with More Able Children

Rosemary Ayles

Introduction

All teachers in mixed ability primary school classrooms work with able children and many feel inadequately prepared for the challenge this presents. Other chapters in this book address the complex task of managing children's learning so that each child in a class is well motivated and makes optimum progress. These are relevant to working with all children, including the most able.

Here we will focus particularly on additional strategies to meet the needs of more able children. There is a considerable body of research into the effectiveness of approaches to teaching children who are less able or have particular disabilities. However, classroom strategies for more able children are not so well documented and, until recently, research has focused on identification and types of provision rather than on classroom practice. Terminology has changed over the years, reflecting changes in educational thinking and practice.

Early studies (Terman and Oden, 1951; Guilford, 1959) defined the gifted as those achieving exceptionally high scores on intelligence tests. Typically the term gifted was reserved for those scoring in the top 1 per cent. Later work (Getzels and Jackson, 1962; Hudson, 1968; Vernon, 1964; Wallach and Kogan, 1965) introduced the notion of convergent and divergent thinking, and broadened the definition to include creativity.

At the same time, teachers in Canada were encouraged to identify highly able children by using observational check-lists. Laycock's check-list, imported from Toronto, was first promoted in England by the School Psychological Service of West Sussex County Council and is still in use. Laycock's work is of particular interest because it marks a shift from research into the characteristics of a very small group of children (not more than 1 per cent, with some studies concentrating on the top 0.1 per cent) to an interest in classroom-based identification of any child showing particular ability or aptitude. This in turn reflects a move from identification for its own sake to identification in order to provide appropriate teaching (Laycock, 1957).

The report of a recent HMI survey suggests that, while there is now no generally accepted definition of an able child, criteria will include a high level of performance on one or more of the following: 'general intellectual ability, specific aptitude for one or more subjects, creative or productive thinking, leadership qualities, ability in creative or performing arts and psychomotor ability' (HMI, 1992, p1).

It would, however, be inappropriate to talk in terms of precise measurement and cut-off points. In practical terms children who stand out as different from others in their class, by virtue of relatively high levels on any of the criteria listed above are likely to present a particular challenge to the teacher. Thus, for example, a child with an IQ of 120, or attainment levels ahead of chronological age in one or more subjects may well need special consideration if no one else in the class has an IQ above 100, or above average attainment levels. In another class a child of similar ability may be one among a number of children who are functioning at even higher levels. For the purposes of this chapter, more able children are defined as those with potential to do well, even exceptionally well, in some areas.

A study commissioned by the DES in the early 1970s reported widespread underachievement amongst the most able pupils. The authors also suggested that the proportion of able children who went unrecognised was: 'considerable, particularly among children coming from poor families, those living in educational priority areas, and immigrants' (Hoyle and Wilks, 1974, p5).

Almost twenty years later HMI reported an increased awareness of able children and of their need for appropriate consideration, but criticised the low level of expectations of such pupils in many schools (HMI, 1992). In the same year the White Paper *Choice and Diversity* in setting out the expectation that schools should provide for children of all abilities explicitly included the more able (DfE, 1992). It has long been recognised that the educational vulnerability of able children arises in part from the ease with which significant underachievement can occur without detection. This in turn can lead to frustration, boredom and, for some, emotional and behavioural problems (Freeman, 1979; Kellmer-Pringle, 1970).

The White Paper *Choice and Diversity* was followed in 1993 by DfE Circular 14/93 which states that: 'Newly qualified teachers should have acquired in initial training the necessary foundation to develop...the ability to recognise diversity of talent including that of gifted pupils' (DfE, 1993, p17).

In support of the clear implication for the continuing development of teachers, central funding was made available for a project to establish a series of regional support networks for teachers, and, for one year only, in-service courses for teachers with responsibility for co-ordinating a school policy for more able children. These were essentially practical measures and their outcomes will be discussed later.

The National Curriculum Council and, more recently, the School Curriculum and Assessment Authority have always given recognition to the particular needs of more able children. For example, it was made explicit in the original National Curriculum requirements for science that: 'Provided that by the end of each key stage pupils complete the statutory programmes of study, higher achieving pupils may be given work above the specified range of levels for the key stage' (DfE, 1991, p3).

A more broadly enabling statement is included in the revised National Curriculum documents which came into effect on 1 August 1995. These include a common requirement for all programmes of study that: 'For the small number of pupils who may need the provision, material may be selected from earlier *or later* key stages where this is necessary to enable individual pupils to progress and demonstrate achievement. Such materials should be presented in contexts suitable to the pupil's age' (DfE, 1995, p1).

There has been criticism that this statement does not go far enough and will be read by teachers as referring primarily to less able pupils (Lambert, 1995). Such a view confuses the place of brief outline requirements which enable differentiation for the more able, with more detailed guidance on how to achieve this. The latter would have no place in a document which clearly states that: 'What should be taught is now statutorily defined; how it is to be taught should be decided by individual schools' (SCAA, 1994, p7). How and when material is selected from earlier or later key stages is for teachers to decide, drawing on evidence from research to inform their professional judgement.

There is a clear link between these National Curriculum requirements and the new Framework for the Inspection of Schools which now requires inspectors to judge the extent to which a school:

- complies with the National Curriculum regulations
- meets the needs of all pupils whatever their age, *ability*, gender, ethnicity, or special educational need.

Included in the criteria for evaluating Teaching and Assessment is the extent to which 'expectations are high and pupils are challenged according to their abilities and needs' (OFSTED, 1995, p20).

Conversely, low expectations are among the characteristics listed for a failing school.

There is, therefore, general agreement on a broad inclusive definition of more able children, and a formal requirement of schools to identify and meet the particular needs of such children. Research evidence on how to do this is patchy. In 1968 a DES report on educating gifted children concluded: 'we need(ed) an increased volume of research' (DES, 1968, p4). The volume has certainly increased, but until recently there has been scant focus on classroom practice.

Recent research

Three studies conducted in the 1970s have been particularly influential. The first (Kellmer-Pringle, 1970) set out to investigate, through analysis of case study notes, the reasons why able children fail, or are misfits, at school. The subjects were a group of 103 children, who were referred for psychological assessment having some form of learning difficulty. Two-thirds were at primary school. The average IQ was 134, with a minimum of 120. Fewer than 50 per cent of the children were regarded by their teachers as of above average ability and 84 per cent were found to be underachieving by at least two years in two or more basic subjects.

Most had not been identified as underachieving but were causing concern on account of emotional and behavioural problems. The complex aetiological factors which emerged included a wide range of mainly family-related factors. A factor of particular interest in the context of this book was that both parents and teachers had inappropriate expectations of educational progress. Parents tended to expect too much and teachers too little. This study was based on a small, highly selected group, and the findings must therefore be treated with caution. It does, however, spotlight two important issues: the generally negative effects of emotional problems on children's learning, and the particular difficulty in detecting significant underachievement among able pupils. For example, a child with a reading level at, or about, the national average, will not immediately cause concern unless there are other indicators which suggest high ability, yet the degree of personal underachievement may be considerable. This under-recognition of ability is an important factor in the development of emotional difficulties in children.

A larger-scale investigation followed, using data on 238 eleven year olds selected from the 17,000 children in the National Children's Bureau longitudinal study who were born during one week in 1958 (Hitchfield, 1973). The children were selected on three criteria: high attainment in reading, high attainment in arithmetic, and high scores on the

Goodenough Draw-a-Man Test, at age seven years. To improve the balance of representation across social groups, additional children from social classes four and five were included. Each child was given a detailed psychological assessment, parents were interviewed, and teachers' ratings were used.

On the Wechsler Intelligence Scale for Children scores ranged from 150+ to 90 with a median score of 129. Teachers' ratings placed 75 per cent of the group in the top 30 per cent on reading, mathematics, oral abilities and general knowledge. Approximately 50 per cent were rated as having outstanding abilities in one area and, of these, 25 per cent were outstanding in two or more areas. There was little evidence of underachievement in the group but this is not surprising considering that of the three criteria for selection two were aspects of high academic attainment, thus providing a sample based more on attainment than ability. However, even with a group selected on these criteria, Hitchfield reported evidence of the adverse effects of limiting circumstances. For example, children with neither books nor access to a library tended to achieve at a relatively lower level than more advantaged children of similar ability, although this was not so in all cases. Hitchfield found little evidence that more able children are provided with insufficient challenge, although doubts were raised by parents and teachers about generalist teachers' ability to satisfy the intellectual demands of the most able 10 to 11 year olds in particular subjects. This may have implications for the sharing of subject expertise between teachers in primary schools.

The third major study of the 1970s was funded by the Schools Council, with a brief to investigate the teaching of able children in primary schools and to formulate recommendations (Ogilvie, 1973). Thirty schools took part, nominated by their Local Education Authorities as providing excellent opportunities for gifted children. Headteachers were interviewed, and staff asked to complete questionnaires about identification, policies and provision, provide a report of their views on how the needs of more able children may be met and compile case studies of one or two pupils. In addition, eighteen study groups were set up around the country. Members of these groups also completed the questionnaires and produced reports of their discussion on related issues. Ogilvie acknowledged that the outcomes are those of a biased group of teachers 'in that it has a stated interest in giftedness'. He also points out that the project was 'exploratory, and suggestions made must be regarded as more or less tentative'. Nonetheless views experienced by the teachers lend support to other studies.

Although 54 per cent of respondents to the questionnaire regarded IQ to be a reliable indicator of ability, most thought that wide vocabulary, imaginative writing, intense curiosity and creativity were also key indicators. 'Lack of opportunity to exercise specific talents' was regarded by 92 per cent as 'possibly harmful to the development of giftedness', and the notion of curriculum enrichment by differentiation was supported by nearly all teachers.

The final report concluded that 'problems of giftedness form a part of the total of those concerned with individualisation'. These included questions of how to provide

- contact with average peers and with those of comparable ability;
- appropriate levels of challenge;
- opportunity to pursue own lines of enquiry and use advanced resources;
- guidance by teachers toward 'a more academic approach';
- access to counselling.

Ogilvie's work, which is most appropriately regarded as a development project based on a consensus of teacher views on what should be done, was influential on classroom practice, and the workpacks produced as a result of the teacher study groups were widely used. It set the stage for a trend in LEA-based projects, mainly dependent on Renzulli's notion of identification through provision. In other words, if the provision is sufficiently broad, stimulating and challenging, children's strengths will come to the fore and areas of high ability will identify themselves. (Renzulli, Reis and Smith, 1981).

The Oxford investigation into the identification of able children in comprehensive schools, conducted between 1980 and 1982, lends support to this method of identification. The effectiveness of tests, teacher-based identification and check-lists were compared. Findings indicated that, while each had something to offer, no single strategy was effective in isolation. Check-lists were found to be ineffective unless subject-specific. Even then they became valid identifiers of ability only when teachers provided planned opportunities for children to gain the knowledge necessary to achieve the check-list criteria. Furthermore, the researchers found that 'teachers could not identify a pupil's abilities in a subject unless the provision was at an appropriate level to challenge the child's abilities' (Denton and Postlethwaite, 1984, p111). The team concluded:

> ...those who seek to make judgements of the abilities of pupils should be encouraged to develop strategies that rely more on the day-to-day clues to ability that pupils display as a result of the challenges set to them, than on test measures of performance. (Denton and Postlethwaite, 1985, p145)

Recent small-scale studies in America advocate a similar approach

(Schack, 1993; Shakles, 1993) while others point to the positive effects of high teacher expectation on children's performance (Brophy and Good, 1974; Goldring, 1990). Other work (Kerry, 1980; Povey, 1980) stresses the importance of good study skills, and some direction and structure provided by the teacher, as a necessary foundation for independent learning.

Several writers (Getzels and Jackson, 1962; Wallace, 1983) point to the importance of building on such a structured foundation by providing problem-solving opportunities which call for risk-taking and stepping outside the conventional. Evyator suggests that 'children will not innovate or travel unfamiliar paths when well trodden paths and established formulae are at hand' (Evyator in Marjoram, 1988, p120).

Maltby investigated another aspect of classroom practice (Maltby, 1984). Her work was based on case studies of 39 children spread across 24 classes in 13 first and middle schools who were identified by their schools as gifted. Classroom observation, sociometric techniques and interviews with teachers, headteachers and children were used. Data from classroom observation showed a significantly higher number of both teacher- and pupil-initiated interactions for the gifted children than for other children in the class. Interactions were 3.8 per cent greater in first schools and 5.4 per cent greater in middle schools than might have been expected if the teacher had divided contacts equally among all members of the class.

This coincides with results from American studies (Good, Sikes and Brophy, 1973; Brophy and Good, 1974) but is in contrast with those of the ORACLE study (Galton, Simon and Croll, 1980) and a later Oxford study (Eyre and Fuller, 1993). In the ORACLE study interactions between teachers and children in three achievement groups, high, medium and low, were almost identical. Eyre and Fuller found that the more able children had little teacher time devoted to them. The differences in the findings may lie in the definitions of the groups studied. Maltby and Good were working with exceptionally gifted children whereas the ORACLE and Oxford studies included a broader group of more able children. It is therefore perhaps the high degree of exceptionality that attracted greater teacher–pupil interaction.

These earlier studies, with the exceptions of Maltby, Denton and Postlethwaite and Ogilvie were not primarily concerned with classroom practice. Their value as a contextual background within which to locate investigation of school-based strategies lies in an emerging consensus rather than the robustness of any individual piece of work. This consensus can be summarised as follows:

- There is a clear requirement for schools to make appropriate provision for more able pupils (DfE, 1992, 1995; SCAA, 1994) and the quality of the provision will be monitored by OFSTED (1995).
- Identification of high ability is best achieved through a combination of tests, check-lists, provision of appropriate learning opportunities and teacher vigilance (Denton and Postlethwaite, 1984; Laycock, 1957; Ogilvie, 1973).
- Shortcomings of identification procedures can give rise to inappropriate expectations by teachers (Hitchfield, 1973; Hoyle and Wilks, 1974; Kellmer-Pringle, 1970).
- Underachievement is difficult to detect and can be considerable (Denton and Postlethwaite, 1984; Kellmer-Pringle, 1970; Ogilvie, 1973).
- Provision of appropriate learning opportunities includes:

  - opportunities to exercise specific talents
  - contact with average and also more able peers
  - opportunity for independent work at an appropriately high level
  - access to adults with adequate specialist subject knowledge

  (Denton and Postlethwaite, 1984; Freeman, 1979; Ogilvie, 1973).

More recent work has sought to address strategies adopted by schools and teachers directly, particularly that of Eyre (1991), Eyre and Fuller (1993) and HMI (1992). These studies will be described briefly, followed by discussion of common issues and implications for classroom practice.

During 1988–90 HMI carried out a series of one-day inspections in schools in seven LEAs where well developed work with more able children was known to exist, and in an additional sample of schools in 18 further LEAs. In total 93 schools were visited of which 36 were primary. Schools were selected from a wide range of locations, including some in areas of social disadvantage. HMI also visited INSET activities and held discussions with officers, advisers and advisory teachers in 20 LEAs. It was not the intention to conduct a rigorously controlled piece of research, but inspections and discussions were carried out within a standard framework of HMI practice. The validity of the findings derives from this. They are not reported in detail but as a general overview, highlighting examples of 'good practice' in schools and LEAs.

A smaller study by Eyre and Fuller in ten Oxfordshire primary schools investigated policy and practice with a particular focus on Year 6. Organisation of provision for more able pupils, and key issues for exploration, were identified through interviews with senior managers and Year 6 teachers. This was followed by classroom observation of pupils nominated by the school as of high ability. The observations set out to 'establish evidence of links between policy and practice; identify particular methods or approaches which seemed to be effective in challenging more able pupils' (Eyre and Fuller, 1993, p1).

In an earlier development project, teachers of 5 to 7 year olds from 12 schools in Oxfordshire identified what they saw as the main issues in making appropriate provision for more able pupils at National Curriculum Key Stage 1, followed by development, trialling and evaluation of appropriate strategies.

Findings of the HMI survey and Eyre and Fuller studies are broadly in line with other work discussed earlier in this chapter. From them it is possible to identify factors which appear to enhance the effectiveness of schools and teachers in providing for more able children. This can be summarised in terms of school level and classroom level processes.

School strategies

Policies, guidelines and co-ordination

In schools general reference to provision for pupils of all abilities is widespread. However, a particular reference to more able pupils, supported by a clear policy and guidelines for systematically planned differentiation is rare. Where it does exist and practice is driven by a policy which is continuously reviewed and developed, expectations for able pupils, and indeed for all pupils, tend to be higher.

Policies and guidelines which are developed and agreed by teachers give formal recognition to practice which may already occur in an ad hoc way. This leads to a greater sharing of skills and purpose across the school and a more comprehensive approach. One teacher in a school with a recently developed policy for identification of individual abilities, and differentiated teaching to encourage strengths is quoted as saying:

> I find that I now look at every child for indications of exceptional potential and I am constantly amazed by the abilities I am discovering. I believe that I am now expecting more and they are living up to my expectations. (Shakles, 1993, p109)

Allocation of responsibility for co-ordination of provision to an identified member of staff, particularly where this is seen as a position of high status which is integral to curriculum development throughout the school, often leads to increased awareness, more systematic identification and improved opportunities for the more able.

Of 486 lessons observed in schools with well developed provision for more able children, HMI judged 84 per cent to be 'at least satisfactory' and 51 per cent 'good or very good'. The overall figures for the same period, quoted in the Annual Report of HM Senior Chief Inspector of Schools are 70 per cent 'at least satisfactory' and 33 per cent 'good or very good'.

HMI conclude 'in those schools which had given attention to the needs of the very able the quality of teaching and learning for all pupils was often enhanced' (HMI, 1992, p16). Other work by Schack (1993) and Denton and Postlethwaite (1985) supports this claim.

Differentiation in the classroom

HMI observations suggested that matching the work children do to their differing abilities is generally undertaken by teachers through four broad strategies:

- *by outcome*, where expectations of response to a common task may be set at a range of levels
- *by rate of progress*, where pupils move through a programme of work at their own speed
- *by enrichment*, providing pupils with additional tasks which broaden or deepen skills and understanding
- *by setting different tasks*, requiring higher levels of work within a common curricular theme or topic. (HMI, 1992.)

Research by Denton and Postlethwaite, and Eyre and Fuller has also shown that teachers who plan specific differentiated tasks as an integral part of the scheme of work in each curriculum area appear to have greater success in retaining pupil interest and motivation, and in pitching work at a level which builds on and extends current skills and understanding. Where differentiation uses only the first three strategies the curriculum plan tends to be less well organised and lacking in continuity. (Denton and Postlethwaite, 1985; Eyre and Fuller, 1993; HMI, 1992.)

An example of a development project drawing on all four strategies is Casey and Koshy's (1995) Bright Challenge Project which investigated how effective provision can be made within the classroom for able and exceptionally able children with special reference to 7 to 11 year old children. The authors found that by designing activities with simple starting points with potential for higher levels of thinking, the whole class can be involved in the same project without having to remove the brighter children for 'extra' provision. Creativity and risk-taking were features of all the activities. The activities were designed with National Curriculum starting points with opportunities for individual enquiry built into them. Results from the pilot trials showed that children were highly motivated, produced their best and felt they were challenged. Teachers found that observing children working on such activities offered them an effective strategy for identification of able and exceptionally able children. Unusual abilities and talents were observed in children who were hitherto not thought to be 'very able'. The class-based enrichment proved effective also in that the work habits and standard of work of all children improved.

Two key issues raised by teachers time and again when considering differentiation are 'managing teacher time' and 'specialist subject knowledge'. Observational studies indicate that careful planning and ordering of tasks, materials and routines are an essential foundation to creating time for a differentiated approach. In addition teaching which aims to help children achieve competence and independence at increasingly high levels of enquiry serves to release them from an overly close dependence on teacher assistance.

Specialist subject knowledge is raised as an issue particularly in Year 6. Effective provision for more able pupils across all nine National Curriculum subjects is rare (Eyre and Fuller, 1993) yet children often have subject-specific talents which require considerable teacher expertise and knowledge if they are to flourish. There is evidence that some teachers of older primary school children, while being aware of their limited subject knowledge in some areas feel that generalist teachers can target each child's needs more accurately. Others take the view that there is room for more specialist teaching in Year 6. This is a much debated issue, worthy of further investigation.

Resources for learning

Good management of appropriate resources can undoubtedly enhance learning. From the work of Denton and Postlethwaite, Eyre and Fuller, and HMI we can conclude that resource issues which emerge as particularly relevant to the needs of more able children revolve around the notion of a high quality environment which nurtures independent enquiry and provides glimpses of excellence. Chief among these are:

- *Staff library*, which should include subject specific texts at the teachers' level as well as books of general strategy and resource ideas.
- *Children's library*, to include a wide range of attractive well indexed subject-related texts to encourage independent enquiry, together with appropriate CD–ROM software.
- *Human resources*
  - ways of sharing teacher subject expertise within, and in the case of small schools, between schools
  - effective use of adults from outside the school
  - encouragement for teachers to maintain actively their own extracurricular interests to a high level
  - facilitation of extracurricular activities for pupils.

It is only on such a well structured foundation where, within an overall scheme of work:

- pupils understand the framework and requirements of each task
- have the resources and skills to complete it and
- understand how it will be evaluated

that Renzulli's notion of 'making giftedness' by exposing children to areas of potential interest and encouraging creativity can thrive.

Classroom strategies for effective differentiation

This final section draws together middle range strategies for effective teaching which have evolved over time from research and development projects. Strategies discussed in earlier chapters for managing learning and behaviour in classrooms are a necessary underpinning to specific consideration of good practice for more able children. What follows should not therefore been read in isolation, but rather as an appendix to Chapters 2 to 6.

Underachievement

It is crucial to keep in mind how easily the most able pupils can remain unrecognised and consequently underachieve without detection. Children from disadvantaged backgrounds, with emotional problems or with a disability (e.g. hearing loss or clumsiness) are particularly vulnerable. A keen vigilance for any sign of talent is vital, together with ingenuity in encouraging its development.

Identification

An inclusive approach, drawing on all available knowledge about each child, is the most positive and reliable. This will include:

- teacher observations of pupils' performance in each subject area, and particularly on tasks designed to present a challenge;
- information on extracurricula activities and interests;
- results of SATs;
- any other information available to the school.

It may also include:

- results of other tests administered by the school (e.g. group tests of attainment or ability);
- results of externally administered tests (e.g. by an educational psychologist);
- information from check-lists.

Information from check-lists should be used with caution. Check-lists are best used first as prompts to the teacher to provide opportunities for children to achieve the check-list criteria and only secondly for identification. (Many LEAs provide check-lists and some make them available to teachers nationally, e.g. Devon, Hampshire, West Sussex.)

Identification is a continuous process whose aim should be to pick up signals of the best abilities of all children. The more able in whatever sphere, will then become easily recognised.

Teaching and learning

OFSTED inspection criteria require teaching methods to be matched to curriculum objectives and to the needs of all pupils. This calls for planned differentiation within an overarching curriculum framework.

Within this framework, **scaffolding** may be used as an appropriate model for differentiated teaching. Originally put forward by Vygotsky and used by Wood in 1976 as a model for increasing intellectual challenge in classrooms, it is summarised by Webster et al. as 'the complex set of interactions through which adults guide and promote children's thinking' (Webster, Beveridge and Reed, 1995, p180).

These interactions are highly influential in children's learning and require sensitive timing, pacing and pitching by the teacher to lead children towards increasing control over their own learning. Webster suggests that by using scaffolding 'teachers can help children to achieve competence quickly, and in so doing gain valuable insights into adult ways of proceeding and managing learning which can then be applied generally to new situations' (p100). Thus the teacher gradually hands over responsibility for problem-solving to the child, and the teaching function recedes as 'the child becomes more independent in adapting procedures and achieving solutions'.

Scaffolding can be applied to any curriculum area at any level. An example of its development in the context of the literacy curriculum is reproduced in Figure 9.1.

It is a particularly appropriate framework for more able children in that it includes high conceptual levels, and readily adapts to the inclusion of tasks which anticipate the next National Curriculum Key Stage. An

Figure 9.1: Components of Scaffolding

1. Recruitment and Management (to task) (Recruiting children to the topic in hand) Gaining attention Directing to resources Directing behaviour Giving personal information Monitoring and checking Prioritising progress through task
2. Representation and Clarification (onto task) **(Helping children to represent tasks in terms they understand)** Adding information Identifying problems Exploratory questions Procedural questions Paraphrasing Reminding Modelling
3. Elaboration (in task) **(Elaborating concepts to make links with existing conceptual frameworks)** Locating and weighting evidence Feedback during task Marking critical features Routes: alternative way of proceeding Assessing need for additional support Taking stock: revisiting nature of task Bridging: finding analogies, parallels and links Maintaining child in field of enquiry
4. Mediation (through Print/Text) (about task) **(Mediating ideas through different forms)** Selecting appropriate formats and written genres Finding ways with words Thinking dialogues Strategic listening to learners' accounts Meeting conventions
5. Finishing (after words) **(Finishing an enquiry through some form of review of the process of learning and its outcomes)** Celebrating, displaying, storing, sampling Selecting the valuable Publishing Convening (drawing together) Reflecting on process and worth

(From Webster, Beveridge and Reed, 1995. Reproduced by permission) example from the literacy curriculum is apt because of the key roles of language and literacy in the acquisition of skills for independent learning in all curriculum subjects.

Grouping

The evidence suggests that children benefit from working in different groupings according to the nature of the task. More able children need opportunities to work with others of high ability, particularly when following a developed interest or working on a task which demands an advanced level of conceptual understanding. At other times the sharing of a range of tasks in a mixed ability group is important for full integration into the class.

Resources and ideas

Building higher level tasks into the curriculum in all subjects demands much of an individual teacher. It is important, therefore, to create a network of support and a bank of sources of materials and ideas.

Within the school, subject expertise can be shared and the advice of the co-ordinator for more able pupils used. The National Association for Curriculum Enrichment (NACE) has a list of regional teacher support networks established as part of the NACE/DfE project. Universities often provide activities such as Christmas lectures and mathematics master classes. Colleges specialising in, for example, drama, music or art may well have schemes to involve primary school children, and senior schools are a rich source of subject expertise. Parents and members of the local community often have a wealth of experience to offer in extracurricular activities and also within the curriculum. The guidelines for more able children produced by LEA advisory services often include lists of appropriate resources.

Finally, it will have become apparent that there is no evidence for a separate set of strategies for more able children. Success lies in the individualisation of strategies which inform excellent teaching for all children. The call for more research into the education of able children has come repeatedly from central government since 1968 and was sent from the Council of Europe to all European Governments in 1992. It is, however, not just 'more research' that is needed, but a sharpening of focus on what actually happens in classrooms and how, should it prove appropriate, opportunities for learning can be enhanced for the more able.

CHAPTER 10

Teaching and Research

Paul Croll

In the opening chapter of this book we argued for the importance of relating what teachers do in classrooms to educational outcomes for children. In particular, it was argued that there are substantial differences between educational outcomes associated with aspects of classroom processes and that a major function of educational research is to identify the relationships between educational processes and educational outcomes. In Chapters 2 to 9 we have discussed research evidence relevant to a variety of aspects of effective teaching in primary classrooms. Although the focus of the various chapters has been different, they have in common a concern with educational activities directed towards outcomes, mainly to do with pupil learning but also including pupil behaviour, and a concern with strategies which are available to teachers in the primary classroom.

The importance of research evidence of this kind for teaching relates to the argument that teaching is not merely a practical skill, acquired through experience, but is also a thoughtful and knowledgeable activity and that pedagogic decisions should be informed by careful analysis and conceptualisation and by extensive empirical evidence. It is in the emphasis on the importance of empirical evidence gathered in a systematic, controlled and replicable fashion and directed towards relating teaching processes to measurable outcomes that the analyses presented here differ from some other attempts to relate teaching and research and to make thoughtful reflection on practice a central concern for teachers. In particular, the account of educational research given here differs from arguments about 'reflective practitioners' (Schon, 1983), claims for the role of 'teacher as researcher' and the approach of action research (for example, Elliott, 1991).

There are three issues which I want to highlight here. The first is the focus on educational processes which are common to teaching situations rather than those which are particular and individual. Second, and linked to this, we have focused on research which is public, generalisable and replicable, rather than that which is personal and specific to individual teaching situations. Third, we have emphasised the importance of educational outcomes as criteria for decisions about educational processes.

As was argued in Chapter 1, crucially important aspects of teaching are common to different teachers and different teaching situations. This commonality arises from a common legislative framework within which teachers in England and Wales work, evidence of common central educational aims among teachers and a common working situation with constraints arising from the nature of classroom life and pupil learning. This book has dealt with aspects of the common concerns of teachers: maintaining order, getting children to work together, balancing individual and whole class interactions, teaching reading, dealing with a range of attainment levels and so on. These are issues for all teachers and a careful study of the strategies teachers use in these areas and the outcomes associated with different strategies provides an important knowledge base for decision-making about pedagogy.

While individual teachers may find value in personal studies focused on their own practice, perhaps using an action research framework, such studies can have little relevance for pedagogic decisions more generally. Indeed, such research typically celebrates the personal, subjective and contingent features of their inquiries and the message for other teachers is that they must themselves become researchers and are disqualified from learning from the research of others. I should make clear that I am not criticising the involvement of teachers in personal research or denying the value such studies can have. I am pointing to the overwhelming advantages of studying teaching situations in ways which make the outcome of such work relevant to other teaching situations and of conducting studies in ways that are comparable and therefore cumulative.

A number of commentators have drawn attention to the very private nature of teaching as a professional activity (e.g. Galton, Simon and Croll, 1980). Teachers work on their own in their own classes and rarely see other teachers in action. Evidence for some degree of increase in collaborative work between teachers and the development of 'whole-school' approaches has been seen as an advance on the traditional individualised work situation of primary teachers (Nias, Southworth and Campbell, 1992). The relative isolation of teachers in their own classrooms means that approaches to teacher development which emphasise professional knowledge gained through practice and reflection on personal experience are necessarily limited by the range of experience people have to reflect on. Not all accounts of reflective teaching are limited in this way, indeed, the best example of these (Pollard and Tann, 1993) encourages teachers to consider a wide range of research evidence and other writing so as to have a broad perspective on teaching within which they can locate their personal experience.

We have developed the notion of middle range strategies in order to focus on identifiable features of teaching where evidence on teaching activities can be linked to evidence of outcomes. Such strategies provide ways in which knowledge about teaching can be used to inform particular decisions about teaching. As was said before, such strategies are not prescriptive in the sense of offering a complete teaching package. However, in many of the areas discussed in this book, the research evidence is sufficiently clear to provide a powerful case for employing these strategies.

The relationships which have been established in the research studies reviewed are probabilistic: they show that two or more variables have a pattern of association but that such an association does not apply in every individual case. This reflects the way that teaching processes are influenced by a variety of factors. Nevertheless, it seems perverse to conclude that because the observed relationships are not absolute, in the sense that they do not necessarily hold in every individual case, that they are not relevant to individual teaching decisions. If one approach has been reliably shown to be associated with more positive outcomes, we surely need very compelling reasons to adopt an approach which is associated with less positive outcomes even if the relationship is probabilistic. Teachers will need to be very sure that they and their pupils will be the exceptions when general patterns of association are established.

In Chapter 1 we gave an example of the situation where method A was associated with 60 per cent success and method B with 40 per cent success. This example was intended to demonstrate that what are statistically quite weak associations (a correlation of 0.2) can look quite powerful for everyday decision-making. There are two further points worth making about this example. The first is that it cannot be interpreted to mean that the 40 per cent of cases successful for method B would not have been successful using method A. There is no reason why the success should not be cumulative. In fact, the evidence considered in Chapter 1 and elsewhere, especially the evidence from the London Junior School project, showed that positive effects are generally cumulative: schools which are associated with greater gains for one type of pupil are also associated with greater gains for others.

The second point has to do with the objection that is sometimes made to such associations that we do not know that the methods are being applied to equivalent cases and therefore that the comparisons being made are 'fair' ones. If method B is typically used for hard cases (children with learning difficulties, patients with very serious illnesses, etc.) then a lower success rate does not mean that the method is less effective. This is a difficulty which can arise with all correlational research although it does not apply to experimental results. However, it is not a reason for ignoring the results of such studies. Just to pose the question shows that we can identify possible sources of non-comparability and subject them to investigation. As long as such factors can be incorporated in data collection their effects can be controlled in analysis. The correlational studies of teaching processes and pupil attainment control factors such as initial attainment of pupils, their social background and other potentially confounding variables. The potentially confounding effects of unknown variables should make us careful in interpretation, but we cannot ignore well established empirical results on the grounds that it might all be influenced by something that no one has ever thought of!

The approach to effective teaching which most of the studies we have considered adopt is a normative or comparative one. The studies are not asking 'What are the effects of teaching?' but 'What are the differences in outcomes associated with different approaches to teaching?' In studies of pupil attainment, all of the classes in each study are typically making academic progress but they are making it at different speeds. The studies attempt to identify the factors associated with the most rapid rates of progress. Similarly, in studies of pupil time on-task, all (or nearly all) pupils are on-task for some of the time. The research has established what makes classes with high levels different from those with low levels. The central point is that, just as with norm-referenced attainment tests, children, or classes, are being judged with reference to one another. However effective (or ineffective) teachers are overall, this sort of approach to effectiveness will necessarily describe some as most and some as least effective. This can lead to the question of whether the differences associated with different approaches really matter, and also to a concern that there is a sort of ratchet effect; however much attainment goes up overall, there will be the same number of winners and losers.

Although the analysis of effectiveness in the studies we have looked at is typically a comparative one, the studies also contain plenty of information on other features of the phenomena with which they are concerned. The evidence presented in Chapter 6 showed how the majority of teachers experience aspects of pupil behaviour in class as highly problematic. These behaviours are not just a problem because other teachers have lower levels of them and the teachers were not making comparisons in describing them. Strategies which successfully reduce such behaviour are clearly of benefit to teachers and other children in their class. Similarly, some of the levels of pupil time on-task described in the evidence in Chapters 2 and 3 seem problematic without any comparisons being made. It may well be reasonable to take the view that new strategies to raise time on-task from (say) 70 per cent to 80 per cent are not a priority and may not even be desirable. But class averages of below 50 per cent time on-task and individual pupil levels way below this are real issues, not artefacts of a system of normative comparisons.

The area of pupil attainment is the one where judgements about effectiveness are most strongly influenced by the normative or comparative nature of the evidence. This is, of course, bound up with the strongly normative nature of the way in which educational attainment is not only measured but also conceptualised. An assessment system which successfully operationalised criterion-based assessments, as the National Curriculum assessments are intended to, would enable us to say not that a child was in a particular position relative to other children but that her or his attainments met certain criteria and not others. In principle, this would mean that effectiveness studies, while still making comparisons (perhaps in terms of what proportion of children taught by different methods reached particular criteria), could also be used to set criteria for strategies rather than simply judge them against each other. The National Curriculum assessments have made some progress here but I have argued elsewhere that it is not clear that criterion referencing in education can ever escape an element of comparisons (Croll, 1990).

While the evidence on effectiveness with regard to pupil achievement is, at the moment, entirely comparative it remains a matter for judgement whether strategies to improve levels of pupil progress are worth implementing. The overall consensus, suggested by public debates over education, claims about the impact of the National Curriculum on standards, arguments about levels of resourcing and class sizes, seems to be that levels of pupil progress and attainment are still in need of improvement. This view seems to be held by teachers as well as by others and is held particularly strongly with regard to the least high achieving children. It therefore seems reasonable to argue that, at least at the moment, comparisons of teaching effectiveness are not an artificial statistical exercise but that a contrast between most and least effective approaches has educationally relevant lessons.

The various chapters of this book emphasise the relevance of research to effective teaching and show that there is a body of research-based knowledge about teaching which is sufficiently robust to inform practice. We have also, we hope, made clear that there is still a considerable amount of work to do in order to more fully establish a research-based pedagogy. With regard to the work of professional educational researchers this work is basically of two kinds. We need to strengthen the methodological base of much of the work we have reviewed. This can be done partly by conventional replication. But we also need to link different types of methodologies in a way that would enable us to attribute causality more securely. This means carrying out parallel work through large-scale surveys which yield correlations, through experimental studies and through real-life interventions where education practice is changed and outcomes monitored. Second, we need to extend research in areas which are relatively little understood. Some of the uncertainties in the study of pupil motivation have been discussed in Chapter 5. We are still uncertain about the effects of class size on pupil learning and behaviour. While this goes beyond the pedagogic decisions of individual teachers, a better understanding of the relationship between numbers in the classroom and educational outcomes is potentially of considerable pedagogic importance. Ideally we should try to combine methodological and substantive progress: the recent class size study in the United States is an example of how appropriate levels of resourcing and political support can result in powerful research designs and potentially important substantive advances (Pate-Bain et al., 1992).

A further potential direction for research which would strengthen the knowledge base on pedagogy relates to the individual studies conducted by practising teachers referred to above. A great deal of thought and effort currently goes into such studies, often as part of in-service work and study for advanced qualifications. At the moment, however, there is little sense of a cumulative body of practitioner research with well established results relevant to other teachers. A way of strengthening such studies is to locate them within the context of large-scale enquiries and to study the operation of the variables used in these studies in particular teaching contexts. If individual diploma, masters and doctoral research studies incorporated benchmark measures derived from major projects this would ensure a degree of commonality in teacher research and would enable the outcomes to be located in wider generalisations about teaching processes.

Effective teaching demands knowledge about educational processes and educational outcomes and the relationships between these. Gaining such knowledge is inevitably a common task for the educational community and demands a thoughtful engagement with both research and teaching. Just as teaching and teacher education needs to be more informed by research than previously, so research needs to focus more clearly on real educational problems faced by teachers.

References

Abbott, D. (1996) 'Teachers and Pupils: Expectations and Judgement' in Croll, P. (Ed.) *Teachers, Pupils and Primary Schooling: Continuity and Change*. London: Cassell.

Adams, M.J. (1990) *Beginning to read*. Cambridge, Mass.: MIT Press.

Aitken, M., Bennett, N. and Hesketh, J. (1981) 'Teaching Styles and Pupil Progress: a Re-analysis', *British Journal of Educational Psychology*, **51**, 170–86.

Alderman, M.K. (1990) 'Motivation for At-Risk Students', *Educational Leadership*, **14**(1), 27–30.

Alexander, R. (1992) *Policy and Practice in Primary Education*. London: Routledge.

Alexander, R., Rose, J. and Woodhead, C. (1992) *Curriculum Organisation and Classroom Practice in Primary Schools*. London: Department of Education and Science.

Alexander, R., Willcocks, J. and Kinder, K. (1989) *Changing Primary Practice*. London: Falmer Press.

Ames, C. (1984) 'Achievement attributions and self-instructions under competitive and individualistic goal structures', *Journal of Educational Psychology*, **76**(3), 478–87.

Ames, C. (1992a) 'Classrooms: Goals, Structures and Student Motivation', *Journal of Educational Psychology*, **84**(3), 261–71.

Ames, C. (1992b) 'Achievement Goals and the Classroom Motivational Climate' in Schunk, D.H. and Meece, J.L. (Eds) *Student Perceptions in the Classroom*. London: Lawrence Erlbaum Associates.

Ashton, P., Kneen, P., Davies, F. and Holley, B. (1975) *The Aims of Primary Education*. London: Macmillan.

Audit Commission/HM Inspectorate (1992) *Getting in on the Act. Provision for Pupils with Special Educational Needs*. London: HMSO.

Axelrod, S., Hall, R.V. and Tams, A. (1979) 'Comparison of two common classroom seating arrangements', *Academic Therapy*, **15**, 29–36.

Bandura, A. (1986) *Social Foundations of Thought and Action*. Englewood Cliffs, NJ: Prentice Hall.

Barker, G.P. and Graham, S. (1987) 'Developmental study of praise and blame as attributional cues', *Journal of Educational Psychology*, **79**(1), 62–6.

Barker Lunn, J. (1970) *Streaming in the Primary School*. Slough: National Foundation for Educational Research.

Bealing, D. (1972) 'Organisation of Junior School Classrooms', *Educational Research*, **14**, 231–35.

Beard, R. (Ed.) (1993) *Teaching Literacy; Balancing perspectives*. Sevenoaks: Hodder and Stoughton.

Beard, R. and Oakhill, J. (1994) *Reading by apprenticeship*? Windsor: NFER.

Bennett, N. (1976) *Teaching Styles and Pupil Progress*. London: Open Books.

Bennett, N. (1992) *Managing Learning in the Primary Classroom, ASPE Papers No. 1*. Stoke on Trent: Trentham Books.

Bennett, N. and Blundell, D. (1983) 'Quantity and Quality of Work in Rows and

Classroom Groups', *Educational Psychology*, **3**(2), 93–105.

Bennett, N. and Dunne, E. (1989) *Implementing Cooperative Group Work in Classrooms*. Exeter: University of Exeter School of Education.

Bennett, N., Desforges, C., Cockburn, A. and Wilkinson, B. (1984) *The Quality of Pupil Learning Experiences*. London: Lawrence Erlbaum Associates.

Biott, C. (1987) 'Cooperative Group Work: Pupils' and Teachers' Membership and Participation', *Curriculum*, **8**(2), 5–13.

Blatchford, P. and Mortimore, P. (1994) 'The Issue of Class Size for Young Children in Schools: what can we learn from research?', *Oxford Review of Education*, **20**(4), 411–28.

Boydell, D. (1980) 'The organisation of junior school classrooms: a follow-up study', *Educational Research*, **23**(1), 14–9.

Boyle, G.J., Borg, M.G., Falzon, J.M. and Baglioni, Jnr., A.J. (1995) 'A structural model of the dimensions of teacher stress', *British Journal of Educational Psychology*, **65**(1), 49–68.

Bradley, L. and Bryant, P. (1983) 'Categorising sounds and learning to read: A causal connection', *Nature*, **301**, 419–21.

Brennan, W. (1974) *Shaping the Education of Slow Learners*. London: Routledge and Kegan-Paul.

Broadfoot, P., Osborn, M., Gilly, M. and Bucher, A. (1993) *Perceptions of Teaching: Primary School Teachers in England and France*. London: Cassell.

Brooks, G., Foxman, D. and Gorman, T. (1995) *Standards in literacy and numeracy: 1948–1994*. London: National Commission on Education.

Brophy, J.E. (1981) 'Teacher Praise: a functional analysis', *Review of Educational Research*, **51**(1), 5–32.

Brophy, J.E. (1987) 'Synthesis of Research on Strategies for Motivating Students to Learn', *Educational Leadership*, **45**(2), 40–8.

Brophy, J.E. and Evertson, C.M. (1976) *Learning from Teaching*. Boston: Allyn & Bacon.

Brophy, J.E. and Good, T.L.C. (1974) *Teacher–student relationships: Causes and Consequences*. New York: Holt, Rinehart and Winston.

Brophy, J.E. and Good, T.L.C. (1986) 'Teacher behaviour and student achievement' in Wittrock, M.C. (Ed.) *Handbook of Research on Teaching* (Third Edition). New York: Macmillan Publishing Company.

Brown, A. and Palincsar, A. (1986) *Guided Cooperative Learning and Individual Knowledge Acquisition, Technical Report 372*. Cambridge, Mass.: Bolt, Beranak and Newham Inc.

Brown, R. (1988) *Group Processes: Dynamics within and between Groups*. Oxford: Blackwell.

Bryant, P. and Bradley, L. (1985) *Children's reading problems*. Oxford: Blackwell.

Butler, R. (1994) 'Teacher communications and student interpretations: effects of teacher responses to failing students on attributional inferences in two age groups', *British Journal of Educational Psychology*, **64**(2), 277–94.

Byrne, B. and Fielding-Barnsley, R. (1991) 'Evaluation of a programme to teach phonemic awareness to young children', *Journal of Educational Psychology*, **83**, 451–5.

Byrne, B. and Fielding-Barnsley, R. (1993) 'Evaluation of a programme to teach phonemic awareness to young children: a one-year follow up', *Journal of Educational Psychology*, **85**, 104–11.

Cameron, J. and Pierce, W.D. (1994) 'Reinforcement, Reward and Intrinsic

Motivation: A Meta-Analysis', *Review of Educational Research*, **64**(3), 363–423.

Campbell, J. (1993) 'The Broad and Balanced Curriculum in Primary Schools: Some Limits on Reform', *The Curriculum Journal*, **4**(2), 215–29.

Campbell, R. (1991) 'Carpet Time in Infant Classrooms', *Primary Teaching Studies*, **6**(1), 85–91.

Carnine, D. and Gilbert, J. (1979) *Direct Instruction Reading*. Ohio: Merril.

Casey, R. and Koshy, V. (1995) *Bright Challenge*. Cheltenham: Stanley Thornes.

Castelijns, J., Damen, H., Stevens, L.M., Werkhoven, W. van and Jager, A. (1992) *Individuele Hulp in de Klas. Bevordered van taakgericht gedrag door responsiviteit. Een programma voor basbsschoolteams*. Utrecht/Hoevelaken: Universiteit Utrecht/CPS.

Cathcart, R. (1994) *They're Not Bringing My Brain Out*. Auckland, New Zealand: REACH Publications.

Center, Y., Wheldall, K., Freeman, L., Outhred, L. and McNaught, M. (1995) 'An evaluation of Reading Recovery', *Reading Research Quarterly*, **30**(2), 240–61.

Clark, C., Dyson, A., Millward, A. and Skidmore, D. (1995) *Innovatory Practice in Mainstream Secondary Schools for Special Educational Needs*. Newcastle: Department for Education and the University of Newcastle.

Clay, M. (1979, 1985) *The Early Detection of Reading Difficulties* (Second and Third Editions). Auckland, New Zealand: Heinemann.

Clay, M. (1993) *An Observational Survey of Early Literacy Achievement*. Auckland, New Zealand: Heinemann.

Cohen, E. (1994) 'Productive Small Groups', *Review of Educational Research*, **64** (1), 1–36.

Covington, M.C. (1984) 'The motive for self-worth' in Ames, R. and Ames, C. (Eds), *Research on motivation in education: student motivation*. New York: Academic Press.

Covington, M.C. (1992) *Making the Grade: A Self-worth Perspective on Motivation and School Reform*. Cambridge: Cambridge University Press.

Covington, M.C. and Omelich, C. (1979) 'Effort: the double edged sword in school achievement', *Journal of Educational Psychology*, **71**, 169–82.

Cowie, H., Smith, P., Boulton, M. and Laver, R. (1994) *Cooperation in the Multi-ethnic Classroom*. London: David Fulton Publishers.

Craske, M-L. (1985) 'Improving Persistence through Observational Learning and Attributional Retraining', *British Journal of Educational Psychology*, **55**(2), 138–47.

Craske, M-L. (1988) 'Learned Helplessness, Self-Worth Motivation and Attribution Retraining for Primary School Children', *British Journal of Educational Psychology*, **58**(2), 152–64.

Creemers, B.P.M. (1994) *The Effective Classroom*. London: Cassell.

Croll, P. (1985) 'Teacher interaction with male and female pupils in junior classrooms', *Educational Research*, **27**, 220–3.

Croll, P. (1986) *Systematic Classroom Observation*. Lewes: Falmer Press.

Croll, P. (1990) 'Norm and Criterion Referenced Assessments: some reflections in the context of the National Curriculum', *The Redland Papers*, **1**(1).

Croll, P. (1996) 'The National Curriculum and Special Educational Needs' in Croll, P. (Ed.) *Teachers, Pupils and Primary Schooling: Continuity and Change*. London: Cassell.

Croll, P. and Moses, D. (1985) *One in Five: The Assessment and Incidence of Special Educational Needs*. London: Routledge and Kegan Paul.

Croll, P. and Moses, D. (1988) 'Teaching methods and time on-task in junior classrooms', *Educational Research*, **30**(2), 90–7.

Croll, P. and Willcocks, J. (1980) 'Pupil behaviour and progress' in Galton, M. and Simon, B. (Eds) *Progress and Performance in the Primary Classroom*. London: Routledge and Kegan Paul.

Cullingford, C. (1988) 'School rules and children's attitudes to discipline', *Educational Research*, **30**(1), 3–9.

Dean, J. (1992) *Organising Learning in the Primary Classroom* (Second Edition). London: Routledge.

Deci, E. and Chandler, C. (1986) 'The Importance of Motivation for the Future of the LD Field', *Journal of Learning Disability*, **19**(10), 587–94.

Deci, E. and Ryan, R. (1985) *Intrinsic Motivation and Self Determination in Human Behaviour*. New York: Plenum Press.

Denton, C. and Postlethwaite, K. (1984) 'The Incidence and Effective Identification of Pupils with High Ability in Comprehensive Schools', *Oxford Review of Education*, **10**(1).

Denton, C. and Postlethwaite, K. (1985) *Able Children: Identifying them in the Classroom*. Slough: NFER-Nelson.

Department for Education (1991) *Circular No. 17/91*.

Department for Education (1992) *Choice and Diversity: A new framework for schools*. London: HMSO.

Department for Education (1993) *The Initial Training of Primary School Teachers (Circular 14/93)*. London: DfE.

Department for Education (1994a) *Circular 8/94: Pupil Behaviour and Discipline*. London: DfE.

Department for Education (1994b) *Code of Practice on the Identification and Assessment of Special Educational Needs*. London: DfE.

Department for Education (1995) *Key Stages 1 and 2 of the National Curriculum*. London: DfE.

Department of Education and Science (1967) *Children and their Primary Schools* (The Plowden Report). London: HMSO.

Department of Education and Science (1968) *Educating Gifted Children: Reports on Education*, No. 48. London: DES.

Department of Education and Science (1978a) *Special Educational Needs*. (The Warnock Report). London: HMSO.

Department of Education and Science (1978b) *Primary Education in England*. London: HMSO.

Department of Education and Science (1987) *Education Observed 5: Good behaviour and discipline in schools*. Stanmore: DES.

Department of Education and Science (1989) *Discipline in Schools: report of the Committee of Enquiry chaired by Lord Elton*. London: HMSO.

Department of Education and Science (1990) *The teaching and learning of language and literacy, HM Inspectorate: an inspection review*. London: HMSO.

Department of Education and Science (1991) *The teaching and learning of reading in primary schools: a report by HMI*. Stanmore: DES.

Docking, J. (1989) 'Elton's four questions: Some general considerations' in Jones, N. (Ed.) *School Management and Pupil Behaviour*. Lewes: Falmer Press.

Doran, C. and Cameron, R.J. (1995) 'Learning About Learning: Metacognitive Approaches in the Classroom', *Educational Psychology in Practice*, **11**(2), 15–23.

Doyle, W. (1984) 'How Order is Achieved in Classrooms', *Journal of Curriculum Studies*, **16**(3), 259–77.

Doyle, W. (1986) 'Classroom Organisation and Management' in Wittrock, M.C. (Ed.) *Handbook of Research on Teaching* (Third Edition). New York: Macmillan Publishing Company.

Doyle, W. and Carter, K. (1987) 'How order is achieved in classrooms' in Hastings, N.J. and Schwieso, J. (Eds) *New Directions in Educational Psychology 2: behaviour and motivation in the classroom.* Lewes: Falmer Press.

Dunne, E. and Bennett, N. (1990) *Talking and Learning in Groups*. London: Macmillan.

Dweck, C.S. (1985) 'Intrinsic Motivation, Perceived Control and Self-Evaluation Maintenance: an achievement goal analysis' in Ames, C. and Ames, R. (Eds) *Research on Motivation in Education: Vol. 2 The Classroom Milieu*. London: Academic Press.

Dweck, C.S. (1991) 'Self-theories and goals: their role in motivation, personality and development' in Deinstbier, R.A. (Ed.) *Perspectives on Motivation: Nebraska Symposium on Motivation, 1990.* London: University of Nebraska Press.

Dweck, C.S. and Leggett, E.L. (1988) 'A Social-Cognitive Approach to Motivation and Personality', *Psychological Review*, **95**, 256–73.

Dyson, A., Millward, A. and Skidmore, D. (1994) 'Beyond the Whole School Approach: an emerging model of special needs practice and provision in mainstream secondary schools', *British Educational Research Journal*, **20**(3), 301–17.

Elliott, J. (1991) *Action Research for Educational Change.* Buckingham: Open University Press.

Englemann, S. and Carnine, D. (1982) *Theory of Instruction: Principles and Applications.* Ohio: Merrill.

Engelmann, S., Hanner, S. and Haddox, P. (1980) *Corrective Reading.* Chicago: Science Research Associates.

Epps, S. and Tindal, G. (1987) 'The effectiveness of differential programming in serving students with mild handicaps: Placement options and instuctional programming' in Wang, M., Reynalds, M. and Walberg, H. (Eds) *Handbook of special education: Research and practice: Vol. 1 Learner characteristics and adaptive behaviour.* Oxford: Pergamon Press.

Epstein, J.L. (1989) 'Family Structures and Student Motivation: A developmental perspective' in Ames, C. and Ames, R. (Eds) *Research on Motivation in Education Vol. 3.* London: Academic Press.

Eyre, D. (1991) *A development project looking at appropriate classroom provision for more able children in Key Stage 1.* Oxfordshire County Council, ACCORD project.

Eyre, D. and Fuller, M. (1993) *Year 6 Teachers and More Able Pupils: a look at the issues in providing appropriate challenges in the nine National Curriculum subject areas.* National Primary Centre/Oxfordshire County Council.

Finn, J.D. and Achilles, C.M. (1990) 'Answers and Questions about Class Size: A Statewide Experiment', *American Educational Research Journal,* **27**(3), 557–77.

Finn, J.D. and Cox, D. (1992) 'Participation and Withdrawal Among Fourth-Grade Pupils', *American Educational Research Journal*, **29**(1), 141–62.

Finn, J.D., Pannozzo, G.M. and Voelkl, K.E. (1995) 'Disruptive and Inattentive-Withdrawn Behaviour and Achievement among Fourth Graders', *The Elementary*

School Journal, **95**(4), 421–35.

Fitzgibbon, C. (1991) 'Multilevel Modelling in an Indicator System' in Raudenbush, S. and Willms, J. *Schools, Classrooms and Pupils: International Studies of Schooling from a Multilevel Perspective.* San Diego: Academic Press.

Formentin, T. and Csapo, M. (1980) *Precision Teaching.* Vancouver: Vancouver Centre for Human Development and Research.

Freeman, J. (1979) *Gifted Children: their identification and development in a social context.* Lancaster: MTP Press.

Frith, U. (1985) 'Beneath the surface of developmental dyslexia' in Patterson, K.E., Marshall, J.C. and Coltheart, M. (Eds) *Surface dyslexia.* Hillsdale, NJ: Lawrence Erlbaum Associates.

Fry, P.S. (1983) 'Process measures of problem and non-problem children's classroom behaviour: the influence of teacher behaviour variables', *British Journal of Educational Psychology*, **53**(1), 79–88.

Fry, P.S. (1987) 'Classroom environments and their effects on problem and non-problem children's classroom behaviours and motivations' in Hastings, N.J. and Schwieso, J. (Eds) *New Directions in Educational Psychology 2: behaviour and motivation in the classroom.* Lewes: Falmer Press.

Fry, P.S. and Grover, S.J. (1984) 'Problem and non-problem children's causal explanations of success and failure in primary school settings', *British Journal of Social Psychology*, **23**(1), 51–60.

Funnell, E. and Stuart, M. (Eds) (1995) *Learning to read: Psychology in the classroom.* Oxford: Blackwell.

Gage, N. (1985) *Hard Gains in the Soft Sciences.* Manilla: Phi Delta Kappan.

Galloway, D. (1995) 'Truancy, Delinquency and Disaffection: differential school influences?', *British Psychological Society Education Section Review*, **19**(2), 49–53.

Galton, M. (1989) *Teaching in the Primary School.* London: David Fulton Publishers.

Galton, M. and Croll, P. (1980) 'Pupil Progress in the Basic Skills' in Galton, M. and Simon, B. (Eds) *Progress and Performance in the Primary Classroom.* London: Routledge and Kegan Paul.

Galton, M. and Simon, B. (Eds) (1980) *Progress and Performance in the Primary Classroom.* London: Routledge and Kegan Paul.

Galton, M. and Williamson, J. (1992) *Group Work in the Primary Classroom.* London: Routledge.

Galton, M., Simon, B. and Croll, P. (1980) *Inside the Primary Classroom.* London: Routledge and Kegan Paul.

Galton, M., Fogelman, K., Hargreaves, L. and Cavendish, S. (1991) *The Rural Schools Curriculum Enhancement National Evaluation (SCENE) Project: Final Report.* London: Department of Education and Science.

Getzels, J.W. and Jackson, P.W. (1962) *Creativity and Intelligence.* New York: John Wiley & Sons.

Goldring, E.B. (1990) 'Assessing the Status of Information on Classroom Organisational Frameworks for Gifted Students', *Journal of Educational Research*, **83**(6).

Good, T.L.C., Sikes, J.M. and Brophy, J.E. (1973) 'The effects of teacher sex and student sex on classroom interaction', *Journal of Educational Psychology*, **65**(1), 74–8.

Goswami, U. (1986) 'Children's use of analogy in learning to read: A developmental study', *Journal of Experimental Child Psychology*, **42**, 73–83.

Goswami, U. (1988) 'Orthographic analogies and reading development', *Quarterly Journal of Experimental Psychology*, **40A**, 239–68.

Goswami, U. and Bryant, P. (1990) *Phonological skills and learning to read.* London: Lawrence Erlbaum Associates.

Gough, P., Juel, C. and Griffith, P. (1992) 'Reading, spelling and the orthographic cipher' in Gough, P., Ehri, L. and Treiman, R. (Eds) *Reading Acquisition.* Hillsdale, NJ: Lawrence Erlbaum Associates.

Graham, S. and Barker, G.P. (1990) 'The Down Side of Help: An attributional–developmental analysis of helping behaviour as a low-ability cue', *Journal of Educational Psychology*, **82**(1), 7–14.

Grolnick, W. and Ryan, R.M. (1987) 'Autonomy Support in Education: Creating the Facilitating Environment' in Hastings N.J. and Schwieso, J. (Eds) *New Directions in Educational Psychology 2: behaviour and motivation in the classroom.* Lewes: Falmer Press.

Guilford, J.P. (1959) 'The three faces of intellect', *American Psychologist*, **5**.

Hart, S. (1992) 'Differentiation: a way forward or retreat?', *British Journal of Special Education*, **19**(1), 10–2.

Hastings, N.J. (1992) 'Questions of Motivation', *Support for Learning*, **7**(3), 135–7.

Hastings, N.J. (1994) 'Enhancing motivation in the classroom: strategies for intervention', *Educational and Child Psychology*, **11**(2), 48–55.

Hastings, N.J. (1995) 'Seats of Learning?', *Support for Learning*, **10**(1), 8–11.

Hastings, N.J. (in preparation) 'The Attunement Strategy in Use: interventions in British primary classrooms'.

Hastings, N.J. and Schwieso, J. (1994) 'Kindly Take Your Seats', *Times Education Supplement*, 21 October.

Hastings, N.J. and Schwieso, J. (1995) 'Tasks and Tables: the effects of seating arrangements on task engagement in primary schools', *Educational Research*, **37**(3), 279–91.

Hatcher, P., Hulme, C. and Ellis, A. (1994) 'Ameliorating early reading failure by integrating the teaching of reading and phonological skills: The phonological linkage hypothesis', *Child Development*, **65**, 41–5.

Hegarty, S. and Pocklington, K. (1981) *Educating Pupils with Special Needs in the Ordinary School.* Windsor: NFER-Nelson.

Hegarty, S. and Pocklington, K. with Lucas, D. (1982) *Integration in Action: case studies in the integration of pupils with special needs.* Windsor: NFER.

Hitchfield, E.M. (1973) *In Search of Promise: A Long-Term National Study of Able Children and Their Families.* London: Longman/National Children's Bureau.

HMI (1992) *The Education of Very Able Children in Maintained Schools.* London: HMSO.

Hodgson, A., Clunies-Ross, L. and Hegarty, S. (1984) *Learning Together.* Windsor: NFER-Nelson.

Houghton, S., Wheldall, K. and Merrett, F. (1988) 'Classroom behaviour problems which secondary school teachers say they find most troublesome', *British Educational Research Journal*, **14**(2), 295–310.

Hoyle, E. and Wilks, J. (1974) *Gifted Children and their Education.* London: DES.

Hudson, L. (1968) *Frames of Mind.* London: Methuen.

Jagacinski, C.M. (1992) 'The Effects of Task Involvement and Ego Involvement on Achievement-Related Cognitions and Behaviours' in Schunk, D.H. and Meece, J.L. (Eds) *Student Perceptions in the Classroom.* London: Lawrence Erlbaum

Associates.

Johnson, B., Oswald, M. and Adey, K. (1993) 'Discipline in South Australian Primary Schools', *Educational Studies*, **19**(3), 289–305.

Jones, K., Charlton, T. and Wilkin, J. (1995) 'Classroom behaviours which First and Middle school teachers in St Helena find troublesome', *Educational Studies*, **21**(2), 139–53.

Karweit, N. (1984) 'Time on Task Reconsidered', *Educational Leadership*, **41**, 32–5.

Kellmer-Pringle, M. (1970) *Able Misfits: A Study of Educational and Behavioural Difficulties of 103 Very Intelligent Children.* London: Longman/National Children's Bureau.

Kerry, T. (1980) *Teaching Bright Pupils in Mixed Ability Classes.* London: Macmillan.

Kirtley, C. (1995) *Rhyme and Analogy card games.* Oxford: Oxford University Press.

Kounin, J.S. (1970) *Discipline and Group Management in Classrooms.* New York: Holt, Rinehart & Winston.

Krantz, P.J. and Risely, T.R. (1977) 'Behaviour Ecology in the Classroom' in O'Leary, K.D. and O'Leary, S.G. (Eds) *Classroom Management: the successful use of behaviour modification* (Second Edition). New York: Pergamon Press.

Lambert, K. (1995) 'Education Review', *Flying High*, **2**, 3–4.

Laycock, S.R. (1957) *Gifted Children: a handbook for the classroom teacher.* Toronto: Copp-Clarke.

Leadbetter, P. and Winteringham, D. (1986) 'Data-Pac: What's in it for Teachers?', *British Journal of Special Education*, **13**(4), 162–64.

Licht, B.G. (1992) 'The achievement-related perceptions of children with learning problems: a developmental analysis' in Schunk, D.H. and Meece, J.L. (Eds) *Student Perceptions in the Classroom.* Hillsdale, NJ: Lawrence Erlbaum Associates.

Little, A.W. (1985) 'The Child's Understanding of the Causes of Academic Success and Failure: A case study of British schoolchildren', *British Journal of Educational Psychology*, **55**(1), 11–23.

Lundberg, I., Frost, J. and Petersen, O. (1988) 'Effects of an extensive program for stimulating phonological awareness in pre-school children', *Reading Research Quarterly*, **23**, 263–84.

Madsen, C.H., Becker, W.C. and Thomas, D.R. (1968) 'Rules, Praise and Ignoring: Elements of Elementary Classroom Control', *Journal of Applied Behaviour Analysis*, **1**(2), 139.

Maltby, F. (1984) *Gifted Children and Teachers in the Primary School 5–12.* Lewes: Falmer Press.

Marjoram, T. (1988) *Teaching Able Children.* London: Kogan Page.

Martlew, M. and Hodson, J. (1991) 'Children with Mild Learning Difficulties in an Integrated and in a Special School: Comparisons of Behaviour, Teasing and Teachers' Attitudes', *British Journal of Educational Psychology*, **61**(3), 355–72.

McNamara, D.R. and Waugh, D.G. (1993) 'Classroom Organisation: a discussion of grouping strategies in the light of the 'Three Wise Men's' report', *School Organisation*, **13**(1), 41–50.

McNee, M. (1990) *Anyone can teach reading step by step.* East Dereham, Norfolk: McNee Publications.

Meece, J.L. and Holt, K. (1993) 'A Pattern Analysis of Students' Achievement

Goals', *Journal of Educational Psychology*, **85**(4), 582–90.
Merrett, F. (1981) 'Studies in Behaviour Modification in British Educational Settings', *Educational Psychology*, **1**(1), 13–38.
Merrett, F. (1993) *Encouragement Works Best: positive approaches to classroom management*. London: David Fulton Publishers.
Merrett, F. (1994) 'Whole Class and Individualised Approaches' in Kutnick, P. and Rogers, C. (Eds) *Groups in Schools*. London: Cassell.
Merrett, F. and Jones, L.(1994) 'Rules, Sanctions and Rewards in Primary Schools', *Educational Studies*, **20**(3), 345–57.
Merrett, F. and Tang, W.M. (1994) 'The attitudes of British primary school pupils to praise, rewards, punishments and reprimands', *British Journal of Educational Psychology*, **64**(1), 91–104.
Merrett, F. and Taylor, B. (1994) 'Behaviour Problems in the Nursery', *Educational Review*, **46**(3), 287–95.
Merrett, F. and Wheldall, K. (1987a) 'Troublesome classroom behaviours' in Hastings, N.J. and Schwieso, J. (Eds) *New Directions in Educational Psychology 2: behaviour and motivation in the classroom*. Lewes: Falmer Press.
Merrett, F. and Wheldall, K. (1987b) 'Natural rates of teacher approval and disapproval in British primary and middle school classrooms', *British Journal of Educational Psychology*, **57**(1), 95–103.
Merrett, F. and Wheldall, K. (1990) *Positive Teaching in the Primary School.* London: Paul Chapman.
Merrett, F. and Wheldall, K. (1992) 'Teachers' use of praise and reprimands to boys and girls', *Educational Review*, **44**(1), 73–9.
Merrett, F. and Wheldall, K. (1993) 'How do teachers learn to manage classroom behaviour? A study of teachers' opinions about their initial training with special reference to classroom behaviour management', *Educational Studies*, **19**(1), 91–106.
Montgomery, D. (1990) *Special Needs in Ordinary Schools*. London: Cassell Educational.
Mortimore, P., Sammons, P., Stoll, L., Lewis, D. and Ecob, R. (1986) *The Junior School Project: Main Report, Parts A, B and C*. London: ILEA Research and Statistics Branch.
Mortimore, P., Sammons, P., Stoll, L., Lewis, D. and Ecob, R. (1988) *School Matters: The Junior Years*. Wells: Open Books.
National Curriculum Council (1989) *A Curriculum for All*. York: NCC.
Nias, J., Southworth, G. and Campbell, R. (1992) *Whole School Curriculum Development in the Primary School*. Lewes: Falmer Press.
Nicholls, D. and Houghton, S. (1995) 'The effect of Canter's Assertive Discipline Program on teacher and student behaviour', *British Journal of Educational Psychology*, **65**(2), 197–210.
Nicholls, J.G. (1979) 'Development of perception of own attainment and causal attributions for success and failure in reading', *Journal of Educational Psychology*, **71**, 94–9.
Nicholls, J.G. (1983) 'The differentiation of the concepts of difficulty and ability', *Child Development*, **54**, 951–9.
Nicholls, J.G. (1984) 'Reasoning about the ability of self and others: a developmental study', *Child Development*, **55**, 1990–9.
Nicholls, J.G. (1989). *The Competitive Ethos and Democratic Education*. London: Harvard University Press.

Nicholls, J.G., Cobb, P., Wood, T., Yackel, E. and Patashnick, M. (1990) 'Assessing students' theories of success in mathematics: individual and classroom differences', *Journal of Research in Mathematics Education*, **21**, 109–22.

Nolen, S.B. and Nicholls, J.G. (1993) 'Elementary school pupils' beliefs about practices for motivating pupils in mathematics', *British Journal of Educational Psychology*, **63**(3), 414–30.

Norwich, B. (1987) 'Self-efficacy and Mathematics Achievement: A Study of Their Relation', *Journal of Educational Psychology*, **79**(4), 384–7.

Nye, B.A., Zaharias, J.B., Fulton, B.DeW., Cain, V.A., Achilles, C.M. and Tollett, D.A. (1994) *The Lasting Benefits Study: Grade 7 Technical Report. Executive Summary.* Nashville: Center for Excellence for Research in Basic Skills, Tennessee State University.

OFSTED (1993a) *Reading Recovery in New Zealand.* London: HMSO.

OFSTED (1993b) *Achieving Good Behaviour in Schools.* London: OFSTED.

OFSTED (1993c) *The teaching and learning of reading and writing in reception classes and Year 1.* London: OFSTED.

OFSTED (1995) *Revision of the Framework: National Consultation.* OFSTED Update, 13.

Ogilvie, E. (1973) *Gifted Children in Primary Schools.* London: Macmillan Education.

Pate-Bain, H., Achilles, C., Boyd-Zaharias, J. and McKenna, B. (1992) 'Class Size Does Make a Difference', *Phi Delta Kappan*, **74**(3), 253–6.

Pearson, L. and Lindsay, G. (1986) *Special Needs in the Primary School.* Windsor: NFER-Nelson.

Perera, K. (1993) 'The 'good book': linguistic aspects' in Beard, R. (Ed.) *Teaching literacy: Balancing perspectives.* Sevenoaks: Hodder and Stoughton.

Pfiffner, L.J. and O'Leary, S.G. (1987) 'The efficacy of all-positive management as a function of the prior use of negative consequences', *Journal of Applied Behaviour Analysis*, **20**(3), 265–71.

Pfiffner, L.J., Rosen, L.A. and O'Leary, S.G. (1985) 'The efficacy of an all-positive approach to classroom management', *Journal of Applied Behaviour Analysis*, **18**(3), 257–61.

Pintrich, P., Marx, R. and Boyle, R. (1993) 'Beyond Cold Conceptual Change: The Role of Motivational Beliefs and Classroom Contextual Factors in the Process of Conceptual Change', *Review of Educational Research*, **63**(2), 167–200.

Pollard, A. (1985) *The Social World of the Primary School.* London: Holt, Rinehart & Winston.

Pollard, A. (1996) 'Playing the system? Pupil perspectives on curriculum, pedagogy and assessment in primary schools' in Croll, P. (Ed.) *Teachers, Pupils and Primary Schooling.* London: Cassell.

Pollard, A. and Tann, S. (1993) *Reflective Teaching in the Primary School* (Second Edition). London: Cassell.

Pollard, A., Broadfoot, P., Croll, P., Osborn, M. and Abbot, D. (1994) *Changing English Primary Schools? The Impact of the Education Reform Act at Key Stage One.* London: Cassell.

Povey, R. (Ed.) (1980) *Educating the Gifted Child.* London: Harper and Row.

Pratt, J. (1978) 'Perceived Stress among Teachers: the effects of age and background of children taught', *Educational Review*, **30**(1), 3–14.

Pringle, M., Butler, N. and Davie, R. (1966) *Eleven Thousand Seven-Year-Olds.* London: Longman.

Pumfrey, P. (1995) 'Reading standards at Key Stage 1 in schools in England and Wales: Aspirations and evidence' in Owen, P. and Pumfrey, P. (Eds) *Children learning to read: International concerns, Vol. 2: Curriculum and assessment issues: Messages for teachers*. London: Falmer Press.

Raffini, J.P. (1993) *Winners Without Losers: Structures and Strategies for Increasing Student Motivation to Learn.* Needham Heights, Mass.: Allyn & Bacon.

Reid, J., Forrestal, P. and Cook, J. (1982) *Small Group Work in the Classroom, Language and Learning Project.* Perth, W.A.: Education Department of Western Australia.

Renzulli, J.S., Reis, S.M. and Smith, L.H. (1981) *The Revolving Door Model.* Manilla: Phi Delta Kappan.

Rogers, B. (1990) *You Know the Fair Rule: Strategies for making the hard job of discipline in school easier.* Hawthorne, Victoria: ACER (Australian Council for Educational Research).

Rogers, C. (1990) 'Motivation in the Primary Years' in Rogers, C. and Kutnick, P. (Eds) *The Social Psychology of Primary Schooling*. London: Routledge.

Rogers, C. (1994) 'A Common Basis for Success' in Kutnick, P. and Rogers, C. (Eds) *Groups in Schools.* London: Cassell.

Rogers, C., Galloway, D., Armstrong, D., Jackson, C. and Leo, E. (1994) 'Changes in motivational style over the transfer from primary to secondary school: subject and dispositional effects', *Educational and Child Psychology*, **11**(2), 26–38.

Rosen, L.A., O'Leary, S.G., Joyce, S.A., Conway, G. and Pfiffner, L.J. (1984) 'The importance of prudent negative consequences for maintaining the appropriate behaviour of hyperactive students', *Journal of Abnormal Child Psychology*, **12**(3), 581–604.

Rosenfeld, P., Lambert, N.M. and Black, A. (1985) 'Desk Arrangement Effects on Pupil Classroom Behaviour', *Journal of Educational Psychology*, **77**(1), 101–8.

Ross, J. (1988) 'Improving Social-Environmental Studies Problem Solving through Cooperative Learning', *American Educational Research Journal*, **25**, 573–91.

Rowland, S. (1987) 'An Interpretative Model of Teaching and Learning' in Pollard, A. (Ed.) *Children and Their Primary Schools*. London: Falmer Press.

Rutter, M., Tizard, J. and Whitmore, K. (1970) *Education, Health and Behaviour.* Harlow: Longman.

Sands, M. (1991) 'Group work in science: myth or reality?', *School Science Review*, **62**(221), 765–9.

Schack, G.D. (1993) 'Development of Giftedness in the Multi-age, Multi-ability Primary School'. Paper presented at the Esther Katz Rosen Annual Symposium on the Psychological Development of Gifted Children, Lawrence, Kansas.

Schon, D. (1983) *The Reflective Practitioner.* New York: Basic Books.

School Curriculum and Assessment Authority (1994) *The Review of the National Curriculum: a report on the 1994 Consultation.* London: SCAA.

Schunk, D.H. (1983a) 'Goal difficulty and attainment information: effects on children's achievement behaviours', *Human Learning*, **2**, 107–17.

Schunk, D.H. (1983b) 'Reward Contingencies and the Development of Self-Efficacy', *Journal of Educational Psychology*, **75**(4), 511–18.

Schunk, D.H. (1985) 'Participation in goal setting: effects on self-efficacy and skills in learning disabled children', *Journal of Special Education*, **19**, 307–17.

Schwieso, J. and Hastings, N.J. (1987) 'Teachers' Use of Approval' in Hastings, N.J. and Schwieso, J. (Eds) *New Directions in Educational Psychology 2: behaviour and motivation in the classroom.* Lewes: Falmer Press.

Schwieso, J. and Ringe, E. (1990) 'Problem classroom behaviour in primary schools: some reassurance from the Federal Republic of Germany', *Positive Teaching*, **1**(1), 18–24.

Seligman, M.E.P. (1975) *Helplessness: On depression, development and death.* San Francisco: Freeman.

Seligman, M.E.P. (1991) *Learned Optimism.* New York: Knopf.

Shakles, B. (1993) 'Preliminary findings of the early assessment for exceptional potential project', *Roeper Review*, **16**(2), 105–9.

Silverstein, J.M. (1979) 'Individual and Environmental Correlates of Pupil Problematic and Non-problematic Classroom Behaviour'. Unpublished Doctoral Dissertation, New York University.

Slavin, R.E. (1986) 'Small Group Methods' in Dunkin, M. (Ed.) *The International Encyclopaedia of Teaching and Teacher Education.* London: Pergamon.

Slavin, R.E. (1990) *Cooperative Learning: Theory, Research and Practice.* London: Allyn & Bacon.

Soar, R. (1977) 'The integration of findings from four studies of teacher effectiveness' in Borish, G. and Fenton, K. (Eds) *The Appraisal of Teaching: Concepts and Process.* Reading, Mass.: Addison-Wesley.

Somerville, D. and Leach, D. (1988) 'Direct or indirect instruction?: an evaluation of three types of intervention programme for assisting students with specific reading difficulties', *Educational Research*, **30**(1), 46–53.

Stainthorp, R. and Hughes, D. (1995) 'The cognitive characteristics of young early readers' in Raban-Bisby, B., Brooks, G. and Wolfendale, S. (Eds) *Developing language and literacy.* Stoke-on-Trent: Trentham Books.

Stallings, J. (1980) 'Allocated Academic Learning Time Revisited: or beyond time on-task', *Educational Research*, **8**(11), 11–6.

Stanovich, K.E. (1986) 'Matthew effects in reading: some consequences of individual differences in the acquisition of literacy', *Reading Research Quarterly*, **21**, 360–407.

Stanovich, K.E. and Cunningham, A.E. (1992) 'Studying the consequences of literacy within a literate society: The cognitive correlates of print exposure', *Memory and Cognition*, **20**, 51–68.

Stanovich, K.E. and West, R.F. (1989) 'Exposure to print and orthographic processing', *Reading Research Quarterly*, **24**, 400–33.

Stuart, M. and Coltheart, M. (1988) 'Does reading develop in a sequence of stages?', *Cognition*, **30**, 139–81.

Terman, L.M. and Oden, M.H. (1951) 'The Stanford Studies of the Gifted' in Witty, P.A. (Ed.) *The Gifted Child.* Boston: Heath & Co.

Thompson, D. and Barton, L. (1992) 'The wider context: a free market', *British Journal of Special Education*, (**19**)1, 13–5.

Thompson, T. (1994) 'Self-worth Protection: review and implications for the classroom', *Educational Review*, **46**(3), 259–76.

Thorkildsen, T.A., Nolen, S.B. and Fournier, J. (1994) 'What is Fair? Children's Critiques of Practices that Influence Motivation', *Journal of Educational Psychology*, **86**(4), 475–86.

Tizard, B., Blatchford, P., Burke, J., Farquhar, C. and Plewis, I. (1988) *Young Children at School in the Inner City.* London: Lawrence Erlbaum.

Topping, K. (1987) 'Peer tutored reading: outcome data from ten projects', *Educational Psychology*, **7**(2), 133–45.

Topping, K. (1988) *The Peer Tutoring Handbook: promoting co-operative learning.* London: Croom Helm.

Topping, K. (1992) 'Cooperative learning and peer tutoring: an overview', *The Psychologist,* **14**(4), 151–7.

Treiman, R. (1985) 'Onsets and rimes as spoken syllables: Evidence from children', *Journal of Experimental Child Psychology,* **39**, 463–577.

Treiman, R. (1992) 'The role of intrasyllabic units in learning to read and spell' in Gough, P., Ehri, L. and Treiman, R. (Eds) *Reading Acquisition.* Hillsdale, NJ: Lawrence Erlbaum Associates.

Turner, M. (1990) *Sponsored reading failure.* Warlingham: IPSET Education Unit.

Veenman, S.A.M. (1984) 'Perceived Problems of Beginning Teachers', *Review of Educational Research,* **54**, 143–78.

Veenman, S.A.M. (1987) 'Problems as Perceived by New Teachers' in Hastings, N.J. and Schwieso, J. (Eds) *New Directions in Educational Psychology 2: behaviour and motivation in the classroom.* Lewes: Falmer Press.

Vernon, P.E. (1964) *The psychology and education of gifted children.* London: Methuen.

Wagner, R.K. and Torgesen, J.K. (1987) 'The nature of phonological processing and its causal role in the acquisition of reading skills', *Psychological Bulletin,* **101**, 192–212.

Walberg, H.J. (1986) 'Synthesis of research on teaching' in Wittrock, M.C. (Ed.) *Handbook of Research on Teaching* (Third Edition). New York: Macmillan Publishing Company.

Wallace, B. (1983) *Teaching the Very Able Child.* East Grinstead: Ward Lock Educational.

Wallach, M.A. and Kogan, N. (1965) *Modes of thinking in young children.* New York: Holt, Rinehart, Winston.

Warham, S. (1993) *Primary Teaching and the Negotiation of Power.* London: Paul Chapman.

Warnock , M. (1992) 'Special case in need of reform', *Observer,* 18 October.

Waterland, L. (1985) *Read with me; An apprenticeship approach to reading.* Stroud: Thimble Press.

Webb, N. (1989) 'Peer Interaction and Learning in Small Groups', *International Journal of Educational Research,* **13**, 21–39.

Webster, A., Beveridge, M. and Reed, M. (1995) *Managing the Literacy Curriculum: How Schools can Become Communities of Readers and Writers.* London: Routledge (in press).

Weiner, B. (1979) 'A Theory of Classroom Motivation for Some Classroom Experiences', *Journal of Educational Psychology,* **71**(1), 3–25.

Weiner, B. (1985) 'An Attribution Theory of Achievement Motivation and Emotion', *Psychological Review,* **92**, 548–73.

Weinstein, C.S. (1979). 'The Physical Environment of the School: A Review of the Research', *Review of Educational Research,* **49**(4), 577–610.

Werkhoven, W. van (in press) 'Improving instruction and enhancing motivation' in Nygand, R. and Gjesme, T. (Eds) *Advances in Motivation.* Oslo: University Press.

Werkhoven, W. van, and Stevens, L.M. (in press) 'Improving instruction and enhancing motivation of low attaining pupils' in Dworet, D. and Bond, R. (Eds) *Thinking Together: changing research and practice.* St Catherines, Ontario: University Press.

West, R.F. and Stanovich, K.E. (1991) 'The incidental acquisition of information from reading', *Psychological Science*, **2**, 325–30.

Wheldall, K. and Beaman, R. (1994) 'An evaluation of the W.I.N.S. (Working Ideas for Need Satisfaction) training package', *Collected Original Resources in Education*, **18**(1), fiche 4, E01.

Wheldall, K. and Congreve, S. (1981) 'Teachers and Behaviour Modification: What Do They Think of It So Far?' in Wheldall, K. (Ed.) *The Behaviourist in the Classroom*. Birmingham: Educational Review Publications.

Wheldall, K. and Glynn, T. (1989) *Effective Classroom Learning*. Oxford: Blackwell.

Wheldall, K. and Lam,Y.Y. (1987) 'Rows versus Tables II: the effects of two classroom seating arrangements on disruption rate, on-task behaviour and teacher behaviour in three special school classes', *Educational Psychology*, **7**(4), 303–12.

Wheldall, K. and Merrett, F. (1984) *Positive Teaching*. London: Unwin.

Wheldall, K. and Merrett, F. (1988) 'Which classroom behaviours do primary teachers say they find most troublesome?', *Educational Review*, **40**(1), 13–27.

Wheldall, K. and Merrett, F. (1991) *Teaching Manual for the Positive Teaching Package (Primary Version) for Effective Classroom Behaviour Management*. Cheltenham: Positive Products.

Wheldall, K. and Olds, D. (1987) 'Of Sex and Seating: the effects of mixed and same-sex seating arrangements in junior classrooms', *New Zealand Journal of Educational Studies*, **22**(1), 71–85.

Wheldall, K., Center, Y. and Freeman, L. (1993) 'Reading Recovery in Sydney Primary Schools', *Australian Journal of Special Education*, **17**(2), 51–63.

Wheldall, K., Merrett, F. and Borg, M. (1985) 'The behavioural approach to teaching package (BATPACK): an experimental evaluation', *British Journal of Educational Psychology*, **55**(1), 65–75.

Wheldall, K., Morris, M., Vaughan, P. and Ng, Y.Y. (1981) 'Rows Versus Tables: an example of behavioural ecology in two classes of eleven-year-old children', *Educational Psychology*, **1**(2), 27–44.

Wood, D. (1988) *How Children Think and Learn*. Oxford: Blackwell.

Wood, D.J., Bruner, J.S. and Ross, G. (1976) 'The role of tutoring in problem-solving', *Journal of Child Psychology and Psychiatry*, **9**(2), 17–25.

Worrall, C., Worrall, N. and Meldrum, C. (1983) 'The consequences of teacher praise and criticism', *Educational Psychology*, **3**(2), 127–36.

Wragg, E.C. (1993) *Primary Teaching Skills*. London: Routledge.

Yates, S.M., Yates, G.C.R. and Lippett, R.M. (1995) 'Explanatory Style, Ego-orientation and Primary School Mathematics Achievement', *Educational Psychology*, **15**(1), 23–34.

Yeomans, J. (1989) 'Changing Seating Arrangements: the use of antecedent control to increase on-task behaviour', *Behavioural Approaches with Children*, **13**(3), 151–60.

Index

(Compiled by Dr Frank Merrett)

Printed in the United Kingdom
by Lightning Source UK Ltd.
106110UKS00002B/421-432

9 781853 463945